# EVERYTHING ABOUT SEWING
# SPECIAL FABRICS
### FROM VOGUE PATTERNS

**Editor**
Patricia Perry
**Technical Coordinator**
Elizabeth Musheno
**Copy Editor**
Alice Rohrbacher
**Writers**
Connie Meyer
Paige Camp
**Artists**
Karen Coughlin
Marilyn Gong
Barbara Hanlon
Janet Lombardo
**Production Coordinators**
Harvey Factor
Susanne Olson

COPYRIGHT © BY BUTTERICK FASHION MARKETING COMPANY
161 SIXTH AVENUE
NEW YORK, NEW YORK 10013

A DIVISION OF AMERICAN CAN COMPANY, 1972

LIBRARY OF CONGRESS CATALOG CARD NUMBER 70-169062

ALL RIGHTS RESERVED. NO PART OF THIS BOOK MAY BE REPRODUCED IN ANY FORM OR BY ANY ELECTRONIC OR MECHANICAL MEANS INCLUDING INFORMATION STORAGE AND RETRIEVAL SYSTEMS WITHOUT PERMISSION IN WRITING FROM THE PUBLISHER, EXCEPT BY A REVIEWER WHO MAY QUOTE BRIEF PASSAGES IN A REVIEW.

# CONTENTS

## Especially For You
**Patterns** .................................... 6
Selection, Sizes
**Fabric** ...................................... 7
Selection, Combinations, Yardages
**Basic Knowledge** ............................ 9
Under Fabrics, Fabric Preparation, About Fit, Layouts, Marking, Basting, Handstitches, Machine Sewing, Seams

## The Classic Choice
**Velvet** ..................................... 16
Priorities, Construction
**Laces** ..................................... 19
Priorities, Construction
**Satin** ..................................... 24
Priorities, Construction

## Seductive Selection
**Sheers** .................................... 27
Priorities, Construction
**Crepe** ..................................... 30
Priorities, Construction

## The Elegant Ones
**Taffeta** ................................... 32
Priorities, Construction
**Brocade** ................................... 34
Priorities, Construction
**Metallics** ................................. 36
Priorities, Construction
**Beaded Fabrics** ............................ 38
Priorities, Construction

## Knit Specialties
**Jerseys** ................................... 40
Priorities, Construction
**Super-Stretchables** ........................ 41
Priorities, Construction

## Special Attention Fabrics
**Ribbed Fabrics** ............................ 43
Priorities, Construction
**Cashmere** .................................. 44
Priorities, Construction

## Trimmings and Surface Interest
**Before You Cut** ............................ 45
**Add-Ons** ................................... 46
**Index** ..................................... 48

# TEMPTATIONS...

The sign of arrival—your fashion embodiment in super fabrics. Making the most of the best puts you in the fabric intelligentsia . . . and accepting the challenges presented by distinctive and demanding fabrics assures your position in the vanguard of creative fashion sewing. An adventurous soul always reaps greater rewards than a timid one . . . and with fabrics like these, why not enjoy a bit of spiritual free-wheeling?

# Especially For You

Super fashions always deserve special fabrics. Whether for a glittering evening on the town, a sportive afternoon, or to satisfy your own creative spirit, you will realize a need in your wardrobe for that dress or ensemble made from a fabric that's more than just a fabric. You don't even have to be the dress-up type—just very specially yourself. The way to achieve that total look of perfection is to select a pattern style that is figure flattering, then make it in an attention-getting special fabric.

We have previously covered some of the special fabrics you may want to use for your creation in the "Everything About Sewing" series from Vogue Patterns—Knits, Fur and Fur-Like Fabrics, Leather and Leather-Like Fabrics, and Lingerie and Loungewear. Here we will concentrate on those fabrics that are special in a more classic way. You will find such feminine favorites as velvet with its soft, plush richness, and lace in all its intricacies. Remember the luster of satin and the rustle of taffeta whenever you are creating a special look. Think seduction in the sheerest of the sheer fabrics or the slinkiest of crepes. Adopt the sensuous look in a body-conscious jersey or stretch knit; surround yourself with the opulence of a brocade, metallic, or beaded fabric. Approach the grandeur of the couture with a luxe ribbed fabric, or try cashmere for the last word in understated elegance. Any one of these fabrics can easily find a place in your wardrobe when you want to put your prettiest and most fashionable foot forward.

You'll want a fabric that suits your personality, besides being simply fantastic in appearance. Don't think you are going to be limited by the pattern's fabric suggestions. Take off on your own fabric tangent by substituting an appropriate special fabric for the pattern suggestions. Use it for the entire ensemble, or mix and match to your heart's content. Try a long crepe shirtdress with a moiré evening cape for a simply dramatic success. Treat co-ordinates along the same line of thinking, and sew up a cashmere jumpsuit with the very sheerest of georgette blouses. You may even want to combine two or more fabrics in the same garment, such as a velvet bodice and chiffon skirt with a taffeta underskirt.

From pattern and fabric selection to construction, everything you will need to know about what makes certain fabrics special and how to handle them is on these pages.

# Patterns

Vogue Patterns has all the special patterns you'll need for creating great fashions from extraordinary fabrics. Our look is special because styling and design have the beautiful life—and you—in mind. For billowy ball gowns, caftans, jumpsuits, sheer cover-ups and lounging outfits —take a good look between the covers of the Vogue Patterns catalogue. Many styles will lend themselves beautifully to special fabrics with a little creativity from you. Let your imagination go while leafing through the catalogue, and visualize what fashion can do for your super fabric, and for you. Select your pattern and correct size carefully to make that design exquisitely your own.

## Selection

The guidelines of good pattern selection are essentially the same for all designs—your goal is a style that suits the occasion, and that is the most becoming to your personality and figure. Do not limit yourself to searching for a special pattern in the evening wear, designer, or bridal sections of the Vogue Patterns catalogue when seeking your design. Many styles from each section of the catalogue can be as special as you want to make them. Let fabric suggestions on the pattern envelope as well as your own fashion sense be your guide when choosing patterns that are not recommended exclusively for special fabrics.

Patterns are often chosen as the fabric yardage and characteristics dictates, as well as by style features. Many times you will search for the perfect pattern after you've purchased a fabric whose beauty proved irresistable. Choose your pattern wisely; fabric suggestions should have the same characteristics as the precious fabric you intend to use.

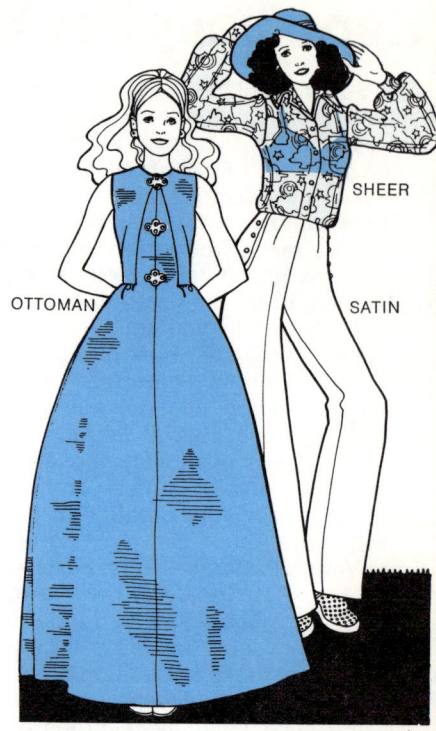

Many designer and evening wear patterns suggest the use of special fabrics and offer additional construction tips for them on the guide sheet. These patterns are most helpful and should be selected whenever applicable to your special fabric and you. If, however, the pattern you choose does not offer such information, don't despair—keep on reading! Vogue Patterns' "Everything About Sewing" series has tips and techniques for creating beautiful fashions from special fabrics.

## Sizes

Choose your correct pattern size according to your figure type and by using the standard measurement chart in the Vogue Patterns catalogue or on your pattern envelope.

Most patterns have adequate wearing ease built into them, but individual styles determine the exact amount you will need. Halter tops, bare bodices with string straps, cut-away armholes, plunging neckline styles, and stretchable knit designs have little or no built-in wearing ease to insure a secure, body-hugging fit. In designs of this type, you may need to choose a size other than your normal one if your bust measurement falls between sizes. Let your body structure and individual bust cup size determine whether you need your regular or a larger pattern size. If your hip is considerably larger than your bust circumference, you may want to purchase two patterns—one to fit your bust, the other to fit your hip measurement. Or, make a muslin and the appropriate alterations. Consult page 11 for alterations, or see Vogue Patterns' "Everything About Sewing Fitted Garments" for fitting information.

## Fabric

Special fabrics are those which require a little more time and concentration when constructing a garment because they have specific structural characteristics. They require special preparation and handling, and employ varied techniques to insure the maximum of their beauty in a finished creation. Velvets have pile, satins have luster, and sheers have transparency—fibers, finishes, and weaves make these cloths as marvelous as they are.

Select your fabric with care—especially if you intend to combine different fabrics in the same garment. In this case, too, plan your yardage requirements wisely, particularly if your special fabric is expensive or if you expect that alterations will be needed. Buy quality fabric—nothing less is worth your time.

## Selection

Choosing the right fabric to go with the right pattern is what great fashion is all about. Your best selection is a quality fabric that is suitable for the pattern design and attractive on you. Use the "Fabric Suggestions" given on your pattern envelope as a guideline, combining them with your practical knowledge of fabrics. You can substitute special fabrics, providing they possess characteristics the same as or similar to those fabrics which are suggested. Weight and texture, as well as the soft or crisp character of the fabric, are important in combining types.

Soft or crisp describes the hand, or feel of the fabric. Soft fabrics fall close to your body, while crisp fabrics seem to have a body of their own and create a silhouette that takes the shape of the design. Many fabrics such as sheers, velvets, and crepes come in varying degrees of softness and crispness, depending on weight, fiber, and finish.

SOFT    CRISP

Quality is essential in selecting fabric, but price is not always a determinant factor. Feel the fabric to be sure—its weight, bulk, and texture are what you must evaluate for your pattern. Check the end of the bolt or hang-tag for fiber content as well as any care factors with which you should be familiar. If the fabric is on grain and can provide what you have a right to expect of it, you have a quality fabric.

## Combinations

Combinations or contrasts of special fabrics for ensembles or within a garment invite your consideration. The Vogue Patterns catalogue has many designs with contrasting bands, lapels, bodices, skirts, insets, collars, and cuffs—use your imagination and create a garment with a combination of special fabrics. Outfits comprised of separates, such as jackets, blouses or tunics, and dresses, jumpers, skirts, or pants, offer flexibility. Fabrics for separates need not be of the same character as they are not joined structurally.

When combining special fabrics within one garment, both fabrics must be similar in fiber, weave, and care requirements. Weight is important, but you can combine different weights in a logical way. A velvet bodice can carry a skirt of ten layers of chiffon. But, a chiffon bodice cannot support a velvet skirt without the aid of a camisole or undergarment made of lining fabric; this supporting undergarment is joined to the skirt with the sheer fabric at the waist seam.

## Yardages

Consult your pattern envelope for the necessary fabric yardage. If your fabric ravels extensively, purchase a little extra and cut 1" seam allowances on all pattern pieces. Pattern designs with contrasting units let you combine colors, different textures, and varied fabrics within a garment. Read the yardage requirements carefully. Your style choice may warrant additional fabric—in a chiffon skirt you may want to include from 4 to 10 layers. Purchase additional yardage if you plan to add more layers than the pattern requires. Figure the length of fabric needed for an added skirt and multiply it by the number of layers you desire. Consider all your fabric choices before purchase.

Not all special fabrics come in the standard widths listed on the pattern envelope. The chart below is to help you convert and ESTIMATE the yardage you will need for a particular width of fabric. The chart makes no allowances for your alterations or for matching designs.

| Fabric Width | 32" | 35"-36" | 39" | 41" | 44"-45" | 50" | 52"-54" | 58"-60" |
|---|---|---|---|---|---|---|---|---|
| Yardage | 1 7/8 | 1 3/4 | 1 1/2 | 1 1/2 | 1 3/8 | 1 1/4 | 1 1/8 | 1 |
| | 2 1/4 | 2 | 1 3/4 | 1 3/4 | 1 5/8 | 1 1/2 | 1 3/8 | 1 1/4 |
| | 2 1/2 | 2 1/4 | 2 | 2 | 1 3/4 | 1 5/8 | 1 1/2 | 1 3/8 |
| | 2 3/4 | 2 1/2 | 2 1/4 | 2 1/4 | 2 1/8 | 1 3/4 | 1 3/4 | 1 5/8 |
| | 3 1/8 | 2 7/8 | 2 1/2 | 2 1/2 | 2 1/4 | 2 | 1 7/8 | 1 3/4 |
| | 3 3/8 | 3 1/8 | 2 3/4 | 2 3/4 | 2 1/2 | 2 1/4 | 2 | 1 7/8 |
| | 3 3/4 | 3 3/8 | 3 | 2 7/8 | 2 3/4 | 2 3/8 | 2 1/4 | 2 |
| | 4 | 3 3/4 | 3 1/4 | 3 1/4 | 2 7/8 | 2 5/8 | 2 3/8 | 2 1/4 |
| | 4 3/8 | 4 1/4 | 3 1/2 | 3 3/8 | 3 1/8 | 2 3/4 | 2 5/8 | 2 3/8 |
| | 4 5/8 | 4 1/2 | 3 3/4 | 3 5/8 | 3 3/8 | 3 | 2 3/4 | 2 5/8 |
| | 5 | 4 3/4 | 4 | 3 7/8 | 3 5/8 | 3 1/4 | 2 7/8 | 2 3/4 |

Reprinted courtesy of New Jersey Cooperative Extension Service, Rutgers, The State University.

# Basic Knowledge

Of course each special fabric has its own unique construction techniques, but there are a few general methods that apply to all of them. These common factors include such things as fabric preparation, pattern alterations, layouts, marking, equipment, and all the basic handstitches and seaming procedures. You may already be aware of many of the techniques that are presented in this section, but think of them now in light of your own very special fabric selection. And, by all means, refer to the section on your specific fabric for additional construction procedures and more specialized information on the basic techniques that follow.

## Under Fabrics

Never overwhelm your fabric—use an under fabric that is slightly lighter in weight. The most important point to keep in mind when selecting any under fabric is to match its fiber content, fabric construction, and care requirements as closely as possible to those of the fashion fabric. Each fabric section will have information to help you choose and use the perfect under fabric for the job it must perform.

**Underlining:** Cut from the same pattern pieces as the garment, underlining is used to stabilize the fashion fabric while supporting inner construction. Some of the fashion fabrics more commonly used as underlinings include batiste, organza, voile, and China silk. Commercial underlinings are readily available in fashion colors in either a soft or crisp weight. Since only the underlining need be marked, it is advantageous to use one with all delicate fabrics as a protective agent against over-handling. Baste underlining to wrong side of fashion fabric sections and then handle both of the layers as one throughout all stages of construction.

**Backing:** The primary objective of backing is to support a delicate or sheer fabric, or to protect your skin from a fabric that is too rough to be used by itself. Backing is cut, marked, and constructed the same as an underlining. Selection is of the utmost importance since the backing must work with and not against the outer fabric. Besides the suggested underlining fabrics, you may use lightweight satin or taffeta, polished cotton, marquisette, tricot, or jersey as backing fabrics. If sheerness is your problem, you may be able to use two layers of fashion fabric in a garment area rather than a separate backing fabric.

**Interfacing:** Stabilization is the name of interfacing's game. It is used for extra support in garment areas like collars, cuffs, hems, and openings, or for a more rigid finish in decorative details. Available in a variety of weights, interfacing also comes in woven, non-woven, and fusible types. Always test the fusible interfacing and bonding agents on a fabric scrap to see if their application makes a difference in the fabric surface; do not use these on any of the special fabrics that are adversely affected by heat, steam, or pressure.

Interfacing is cut from the appropriate pattern pieces or as instructed by your pattern cutting guide. Attach interfacing as directed in your sewing guide. Or, refer to The Vogue Sewing Book for various methods of applying interfacing to eliminate bulk in your seams.

**Stiffening:** Whenever a defined shape is wanted, it calls for a special shaper. These fabrics go one step beyond interfacing to support and control specific garment areas or design features. Crinoline, horsehair braid, heavyweight interfacing, hair canvas, net, buckram, and organdy may all find application here, depending on the particular use and the fabric with which it will be used.

**Lining:** Add a fashion touch and a smooth interior finish with a lining. It conceals inner construction details and lengthens a garment's life span by protecting it from abrasion. Linings may be applied by hand or machine either in an entire garment or in specific areas. Refer to The Vogue Sewing Book for traditional and extra lining techniques needed for your special fabric. Use lining fabric for facings when working with a bulky fabric. Common lining fabrics include commercial linings, China silk, or any smooth fabric of an appropriate weight and opacity.

## Fabric Preparation

The most imperative prerequisites to cutting and construction are getting the fabric on grain and pre-shrinking it. They are related to the pressing and handling procedures that will be required for each specific fabric.

**Grain:** To make sure that a fabric is on grain, straighten the ends of the fabric first, then align the grains.

Follow the general straightening procedure of pulling a crosswise thread and cutting alongside the thread, adapting it as needed for your special fabric. For heavily ribbed fabrics, simply cut along one of the prominent crosswise threads. Fabric with surface texture, like satin or velvet, will be easier to work with from the wrong side. When threads cannot be pulled or when working with knits, mark with pins along crosswise thread or course; cut along the line of pins. For straightening lace fabric, see page 21.

To align the grain if your fabric is only slightly off-grain, pin it in half, right sides together, and press it by the recommended method. Fabrics that are severely off-grain will need to be pulled at the corners in a direction opposite the slant of the ends. Do not use this method on metallic or beaded fabrics, as it may break the threads.

Remember that bonded fabrics or those with certain finishes may be permanently off-grain. You must use these fabrics as they are.

**Pre-shrinking Fabric:** As a general rule, washable fabrics with a residual shrinkage of 1% or more should be pre-shrunk by immersion in water; they are then dried by the chosen method. Dry cleanable fabrics should be steam-pressed. Of course, these generalities may be revised to suit your specific fabric. Because of construction or fiber content, many of the special fabrics are not washable. Read the hang-tag or the end of the fabric bolt very carefully when purchasing fabric and write down all pertinent information. Do not steam-press your fabric if it may be at all damaged by steam.

Note: Before cutting out your pattern, check to see if the center crease will press out; use the pressing technique appropriate for your fabric, and work from only the wrong side. If the crease is still evident, brush with a damp sponge and press again.

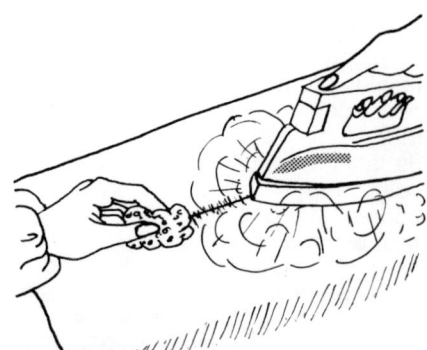

If crease still remains, position pattern pieces to avoid it or place it in an inconspicuous spot.

## About Fit

Take note of the following pattern alterations and fitting procedures pertinent to special fabrics.

**Fitting the Pattern** must precede construction. Make your usual pattern adjustments and alterations; allow 1" seam allowances on vertical seams if uncertain.

**Fitting a Sleeve Cap** is often needed in special fabrics that cannot be eased successfully. When pinning the sleeve in the armhole, smooth the sleeve cap from notches toward shoulder, forming a shallow tuck at the top of sleeve. On your sleeve pattern, make an identical tuck at the top of sleeve cap (pattern will bubble slightly). Make 1½" clips at each end of ease markings so seam allowances lie flat, and shorten sleeve cap slightly. Re-cut the sleeve cap, using the altered pattern piece; add new ease threads.

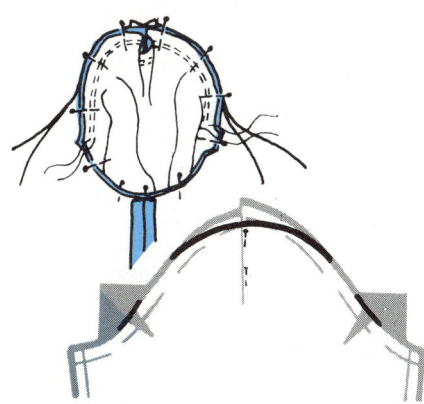

**Fitting Design Details** may be needed for styles like décolleté or halter necklines, or skinny strapped bodices; these have less wearing ease than a basic pattern in the same size. Allow 1" seam allowances and hand baste seams together for fitting before stitching. Or, make the design in another fabric to test and fit it before cutting your special fabric.

## Layouts

Many special fabrics have a nap, texture, design, or sheen. Therefore, they must be cut so all pattern pieces will go in the same direction. This assures uniform coloration and textural effects throughout the garment. Follow your pattern's cutting guide for a "With Nap" layout. If in doubt as to the direction of your pattern pieces, hold the tissue over the correct portion of your body and mark all pieces with a directional arrow. Position pattern pieces on the fabric so arrows go in one direction.

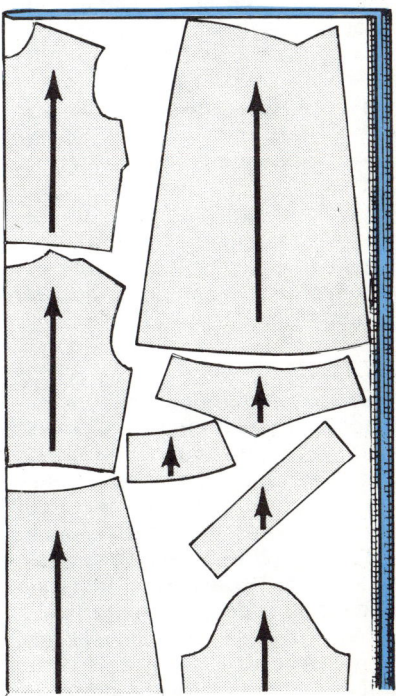

Other layout hints to use on special fabrics are as follows:
- Extend grainlines to pattern ends with pencil; measure often to be sure pattern is on correct grain.
- To avoid fabric distortion, work on a large, flat surface so fabric does not hang over the edge.

- Anchor slippery or stretchy fabrics to the cutting surface with weights; pin to cutting board or pin to a sheet securely anchored to cutting surface to prevent shifting of grain.
- Lay out all pattern pieces before cutting any of them.
- Place pattern pieces printed side up unless otherwise indicated.
- For pattern pieces extending beyond the fabric fold, cut all other pieces first, then unfold fabric and cut remaining pieces.
- Place silk or ball point pins in seam allowances to avoid snagging.
- Cut fabric with sharp shears and steady, even slashes. Never use pinking shears when cutting out a garment.
- Place pattern pieces on wrong side of fabric; pin to one or two layers, depending on thickness.
- Cut all notches outward.
- To avoid crushing fabric, store cut pieces by hanging or laying flat.
- Save fabric scraps to test pressing and stitching techniques, and for garment details.

## Marking

Choose a marking method that will not leave permanent marks on the fabric during application or removal. Always test the chosen method on a fabric scrap for ease of application, pressing, and removal.

**Tracing Wheel and Dressmaker's Tracing Paper:** This fast and easy method is good for underlining, backing, or hard-surfaced fabrics. Choose a color that contrasts slightly with the fabric color; some colors are difficult or impossible to remove. At times the tracing wheel alone is effective in marking fabrics. Be sure that it does not tear delicate fabrics or mar textured surfaces.

**Tailor's Tacks:** Exceptionally good for sheers or delicate fabrics, this method may take a little more time. Use silk thread and a fine needle for best results; test to see if holes are left when tailor's tacks are removed. Use white thread or a color slightly lighter than the fabric.

**Tailor's Chalk:** This method works on nearly any fabric whether delicate or hard-surfaced. Test for removability, since this is the main limiting factor in its use.

**Thread Tracing:** This method transfers your position markings, etc., to the right side of the fabric for easy placement of your garment's fashion details. Use silk thread and a fine needle to avoid permanent marks. Test to determine if pin marks or holes will remain.

## Basting

Basting, done by hand or machine, is a temporary stitch used to indicate markings, attach interfacing, and hold fabric pieces together before permanently stitching. Basting garment sections of special fabrics calls for special handling, as most of these fabrics mar easily. Use a sharp fine needle and silk thread when basting. Silk thread prevents slippage and makes basting of velvets and other dense fabrics easier in fitting and positioning. Use common sense when basting special fabrics: baste in the seam allowance close to the stitching line to keep basting marks out of sight and to make threads easily removable.

**Diagonal Basting:** This is also known as tailor basting and has a variety of uses. It holds facings, interfacings, and linings during fittings, and is especially useful in handling special fabrics during a number of different operations. Many hard-to-handle fabrics need to be basted in place before certain areas can be steam-pressed. Use diagonal basting to secure favored edges—garment arm and neck edges for example—and to insure a properly pressed edge. Be extremely careful not to use diagonal basting in this manner if your fabric shows needle marks or is easily flattened.

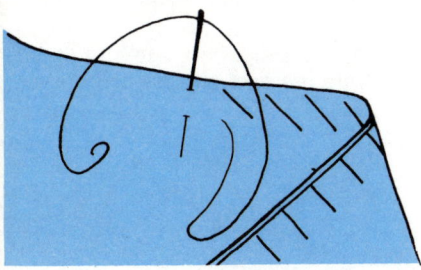

**Pin Basting:** Basting with pins should be limited to those fabrics which do not mar easily. Place silk or ball point pins at right angles to seamline with heads pointing toward raw edge. It is not wise to stitch over pins in most special fabrics, so remove them as you work. Remove pins promptly to avoid imprints.

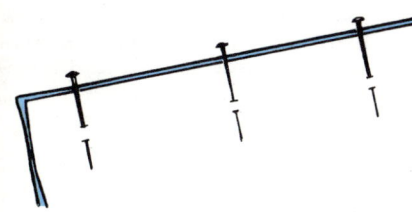

## Handstitches

Unlike basting, handstitches are permanent. Use a fine, sharp needle and either silk or cotton-covered polyester thread for easy manipulation and durable stitches. When hand sewing delicate fabrics, keep thread and stitches loose, but secure, to avoid dimples and wrinkles.

The variety of stitches on this and the following page are those most frequently used in garment construction. Use the SLIPSTITCH for finishing. The BACKSTITCH and HALF BACKSTITCH are handy for difficult-to-control or hard-to-reach areas. A PRICKSTITCH ensures a strong hand-applied zipper. Use the CATCHSTITCH to hem or secure interfacing. A RUNNING STITCH gives you maximum control for gathers and easing. The HEMMING STITCH is used with stretch lace or a seam binding finish. A BLINDSTITCH is for bound or overcast hems, and for holding facings inconspicuously to the underlining or backing inside the garment.

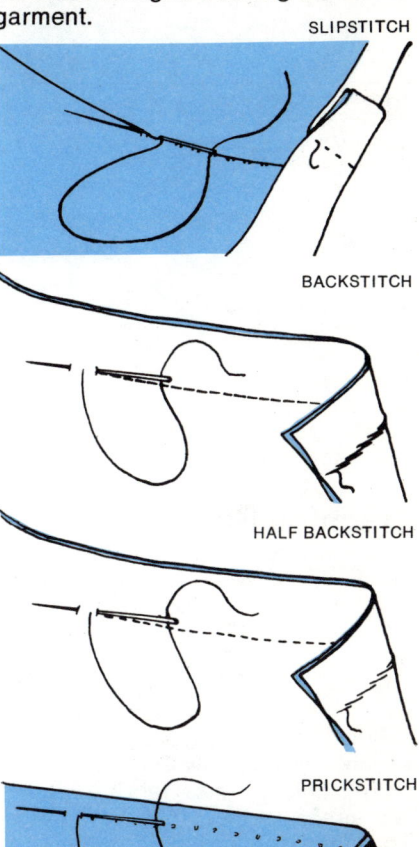

SLIPSTITCH

BACKSTITCH

HALF BACKSTITCH

PRICKSTITCH

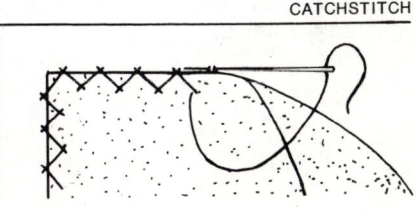

CATCHSTITCH

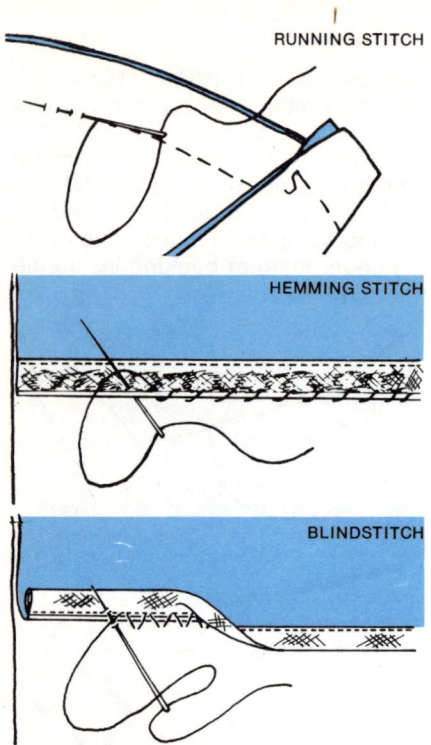

fabric's section in this book—certain seams are better suited for particular fabrics.

Structural seams are sewn and finished as dictated by style and fabric. Curved seams may require notching and clipping to lie flat—notch outward curves and clip inward curves.

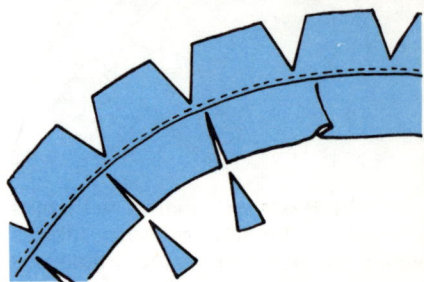

Corner seams need some preliminary preparation—reinforcement stitches and clipping (1). Stitch alongside the reinforcement stitches, pivoting at the corner (2).

Press seam allowances open or as indicated on sewing guide. Catchstitch trimmed edges together (3).

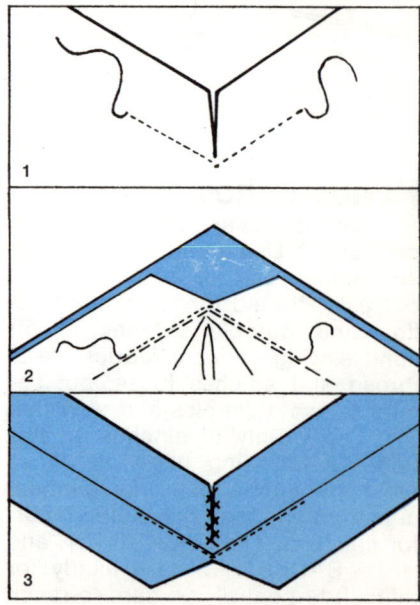

## Machine Sewing

The strength of your seams depends primarily on correctly adjusting the tension of the machine. Tension is correct when both top and bobbin threads are drawn equally into the fabric. Check your stitch length, too, before sewing. Pressure should feed both layers of the fabric evenly and smoothly through the machine. Thick, dense fabrics require less pressure than thin, flat fabrics. Your feed dog and throat plate must be free of rough protrusions to prevent snagging. Machine needles must be sharp; dull or rough needles damage the fabric so check them often. A ball point needle is suggested for knits.

## Seams

Careful, precise seam construction is a must. Tips to help you with special fabrics can be found in the

When attaching a gathered edge to a straight edge, pin matching symbols, adjust gathers evenly, then baste. Press seam allowances together to reduce bulk but do not press beyond the seamline as gathers would be flattened.

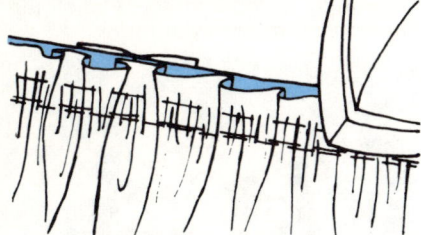

With gathered section uppermost, stitch along inner gathering stitches. Smooth gathers as you stitch.

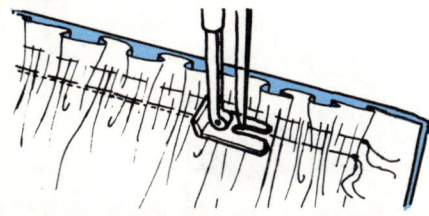

Stretchy knits and sheers are sewn with tissue paper to prevent their being damaged by the feed dog. Place tissue paper on the machine bed under the fabric. Stitch through all thicknesses; tear away paper.

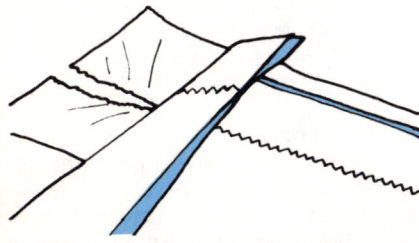

Tape curved and straight seams that will receive the greatest amount of strain when you wear your garment. Pre-shrunk twill tape or ribbon seam binding is used on straight seams, while bias tape—whose slack has been pressed out, and which has been shaped like garment contours —works best on curved seams. Place tape over seamline, extending ⅛"

into seam allowance and anchor permanently when seam is stitched.

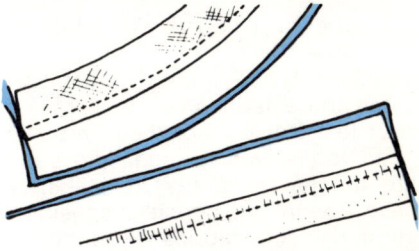

Enclosed seams, regardless of the fabric type, should be trimmed and graded—corners and curves require clipping and notching.

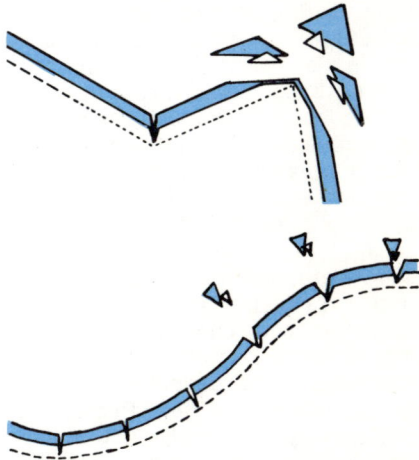

For flat facings, understitch seam allowances to facing along seam after trimming, grading, and clipping.

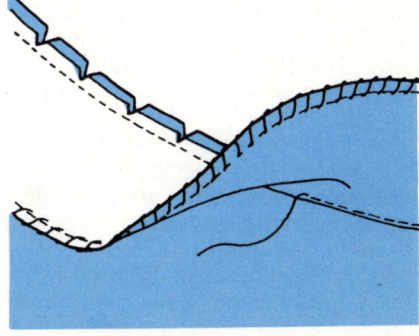

# The Classic Choice

Whenever you think of fabrics that deserve and demand special attention—we're willing to bet that these three fabrics are the first on your list. Because of their versatile good looks, velvet, lace, and satin are the perennial favorites — they have dominated people's consideration of special fabrics for centuries.

## Velvet

Plushy, luxurious velvet is a feminine fabric classic in its own right. During the process of its construction, an extra set of raised yarns is added to a woven or knitted base; these are then cut or left as loops to produce the desired surface effect. The fabrics made in this manner are known as pile fabrics and each has a definite nap or shading due to the uneven reflection of light from the textured surface. To determine the direction of the nap, brush your hand lightly over fabric surface. The smoother direction is the one going with the nap; the rougher direction is the one going against the nap. Pile fabrics are usually cut so the nap will be going up on the finished garment; this produces a richer appearance because the fabric appears darker when you look down into the pile.

In the velvet family and requiring similar handling, are velveteen, corduroy, plush, and velour, as well as the vast number of modified velvets. The hand of these fabrics can be either soft or crisp, depending on fiber content, fabric construction, closeness of weave, and density of pile. Select the correct weight and drapability for your pattern choice. Clingy pannes are great for slinky dresses and jumpsuits, but you'd be better off with a crisp, heavier velvet for a suit or cape. Deep pile fabrics make your figure appear larger, but velvet with a slenderizing fabric like taffeta or chiffon in the same garment is an effective solution.

## Priorities

Getting a velvet garment together with these hints will make construction quicker and easier.

**Under Fabrics:** An underlining is often unnecessary for velvet, but may be a desirable feature since it can be marked, rather than the fabric. Underlining should be of the lightest weight that will go with your fabric. For interfacing and lining, follow standard application procedures. If fabric is very thick, cut facing pieces from lining.

**Fabric Preparation:** Velvets should be handled as little as possible because the pile is easily crushed. Always store velvet by pinning it to a hanger along one selvage; folding will crush the nap. Preshrink velvet by the best method for your fabric's fiber content. Shower steaming removes wrinkles and prepares fabric for cutting.

**Alterations and Fitting:** You will find pattern alterations and fitting tips on page 11. You must evaluate the thickness of your fabric and the number of seams, allowing wider seam allowances due to fabric or design. Fit out any excess ease in sleeve cap as needed.

**Layouts:** Always use a "With Nap" layout. Whether the nap runs up or down, make sure it is the same throughout the garment.

**Marking:** Tailor's chalk or tailor's tacks are recommended for marking velvets. Use tracing wheel and paper only on underlining.

## Construction

The only way to sew with velvet is to learn about and then use the construction techniques required by this fabric.

**Pressing:** The pile of velvet fabrics is squashed easily and may be impossible to raise. Always test-press a fabric scrap before starting even the first construction steps. Place fabric, pile side down, on a needleboard to keep it from being flattened; press. When pile is exposed on both sides, as in a seam, use a self-fabric press cloth on inside of garment.

If you do not have a needleboard, try substituting a self-fabric scrap or a fluffy towel. Or, stand your iron on end and cover it with a damp cloth. Holding the velvet lightly, run the wrong side of the fabric across the covered iron to press seams and steam out wrinkles.

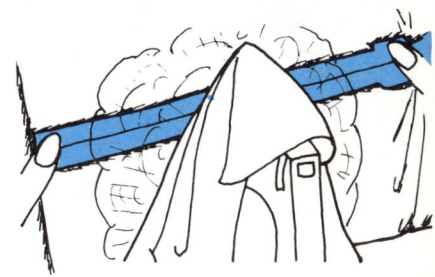

**Seams:** Refer to pages 14-15 for basic information on seams. Baste all seams closely with silk thread before stitching; backstitch every 2"-3" to prevent shifting. Loosen the pressure on the presser foot, and stitch as for a regular seam; hold the seam taut as you stitch in the direction of the nap. When a seam joins a pile fabric to a regular fabric, keep the section without nap on top as you stitch. All fitting adjustments should be made while garment is basted, since machine stitches could leave permanent marks.

Structural seams that need support should be taped (see page 15). If fabric ravels, seam edges will need finishing. For a STITCHED AND OVERCAST FINISH, machine stitch ¼" from cut edge, trim to ⅛", and overcast by hand.

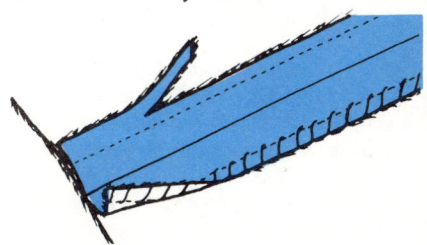

A **ZIGZAG FINISH** is good for fabrics which ravel easily. Adjust stitch width to suit fabric weight, then zigzag near each cut edge.

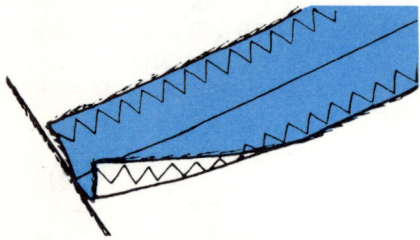

The **BOUND FINISH** is also recommended. Encase each cut edge in a double-fold bias binding, placing the narrower edge on top, and edgestitch through all layers.

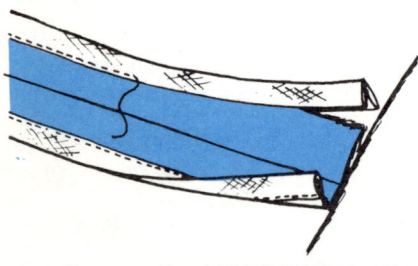

Or, use the **HONG KONG FINISH** (pages 25-26).

Enclosed seams should be pressed open first, then turned in the proper position. Baste turned edges loosely before pressing. Using a self-fabric press cloth and a needleboard, gently work the edges into place with your fingers.

When stitching darts, follow the same precautions as for seams. If fabric is thick or bulky, slash and trim the dart, then press it open.

**Closures:** All cautions and cares should be given to the closure area. When your design calls for a zipper, and you want to use a regular one, insert it by hand using a prickstitch. Unique invisible zippers installed by machine provide a smooth, hidden finish. Buttonholes should be either bound or made by machine; the primary caution here is against over-handling and over-pressing. You may want to substitute loops for buttonholes, or use a decorative closure like braided frogs and jeweled or metal clasps.

**Hems:** The hem of a velvet garment must be inconspicuous and soft. This must be accomplished with minimum handling and pressing, and by using loose hemming stitches that are securely tacked every 4"-5". You may use any of the recommended seam finishes as hem finishes. For straight hems, use ribbon seam binding; for curved or stretchy hems, use bias seam binding or stretch lace.

Many times extra support is needed in the hem area to keep the edge softly rounded and the pile uncrushed. An **INTERFACED HEM** will solve the problem in an underlined garment. Use hair canvas or the like for stiffness, or lamb's wool or flannel for softness. Mark the hemline with thread tracing. Cut a bias strip of interfacing equal in width to the hem depth, and long enough to lap ends ½"; piece if necessary. Place interfacing in the hem area, extending one edge ⅝" below hemline. Sew interfacing to underlining with long running stitches along hemline, and with long, loose catchstitches along upper edge. Turn up hem and baste close to fold. Finish the hem edge as desired and sew the hem in place to underlining.

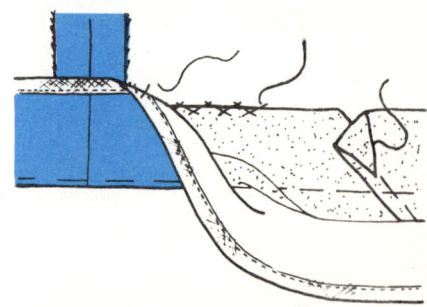

Press, shaping edge in a soft crease or roll.

**Special Touches:** Whenever a heavier velvet skirt is used with a lighter weight bodice fabric, seams may pull and the fabric may tear. Some inside support will alleviate the problem. Cut a strip of ½" wide grosgrain ribbon to fit the waist, plus 1" for finishing ends. Turn ends back ½" and stitch; attach hooks and eyes to the ribbon ends. Sew the stay to seams and darts, leaving 2" free on each side of zipper.

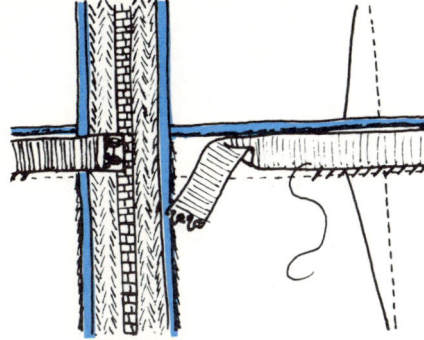

**Care:** Once again you will use the information obtained from the end of the fabric bolt or the hangtag. It is your best guide for the proper cleaning procedure. Most velvets should be dry cleaned to preserve their pile surfaces. Occasionally your velvet garment will have only wrinkles or a lightly crushed pile caused by sitting. Don't feel that you must send it to the cleaner's every time it has become wrinkled. Quite often all it will need is to be hung in the bathroom while you are taking a steamy shower. Wrinkles will disappear, and the pile should return to normal. When a velvet garment is stored in the closet, be careful not to over-crowd it. The weight of another garment pressing upon it can be enough to crush velvet pile. It is also a good idea to use padded hangers for storage and to fill out curves such as sleeves or bell skirts with tissue paper so that they will retain their original shape.

# Laces

Laces, originally made only by hand, have always been valued as exquisite fabric and elegant trimmings. Machine-made laces have duplicated intricate traditional design so well that it is sometimes difficult to distinguish between handmade and machine-made varieties. Man's technology has even produced laces stable enough to take machine washing. The finest laces are linen, but beautiful high-quality laces can be found made from cotton, silk, rayon, and synthetic fibers.

Whether delicate or sturdy, laces require special handling to ensure the beauty of the finished garment. The fashion finesse of lace depends largely on the placement of the motifs of the fabric in relation to the garment design. This is more easily accomplished than you might think. The mesh construction of most laces allows you to work in either a crosswise or lengthwise direction, depending on the position of the motif. When purchasing your lace, check your pattern yardage requirements—lace having a one-way design may not be suitable.

Many laces have a scalloped edge that can be worked beautifully into ruffles, a skirt, sleeves, or a delicate neck edge. Consider how you can use such an edge to advantage in the fashion you've chosen before purchasing your fabric.

The wide variety of laces available include fine openwork laces with delicate appliqués and embroidered motifs, and all-over laces in many designs and colors. Lace fabrics are sold in a variety of widths, and lace trimmings include flouncing for ruffles, galloons with two decorative edges, insertions, edgings, and beading laces to entwine the loveliest of ribbons. For information and construction tips on these lace trimmings, see "Everything About Sewing Trims" from Vogue Patterns.

Lace can be used for an entire dress, or for only a bodice or skirt. An openwork lace can result in a beautiful sleeve or an elegant blouse over a camisole top. Let the weight and density of the fabric assist you in determining the look you want.

## Priorities

A lace creation may take a little more time than those from other special fabrics. The more delicate the lace, the more care must be given in construction and handling of the fabric. Hints for the construction and handling of laces from the most fragile to heavier ones—are on the following pages.

**Under Fabrics:** Some of the most beautiful lace garments have no inner supporting fabrics. When an underlining or backing is to be used, consider one that will not detract from the appearance of your lace. Backing works best on sheer or openwork lace, as it can be of a matching or contrasting color to add another dimension to your garment as well as comfort and supporting qualities. Some laces can be both delicate and scratchy. Backing can be sheer or opaque, or hint at nudity beneath your lace with lightweight satin or taffeta, organdy, batiste, crepe, polished cotton, nude marquisette, tricot, or jersey.

There are two methods for applying a backing to scalloped lace. The edge of the backing may be cut straight and even, with the edge of the backing level to the inner points of the scallops, then turned under and whipstitched in place.

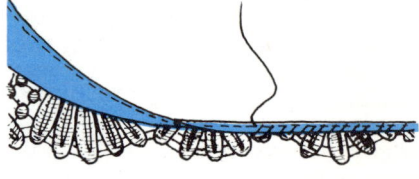

If you prefer to back the scalloped edge more precisely, cut your backing edge using the scallops as a guide. Staystitch the backing scallops ⅛" from the edge; trim. Whipstitch the edge of backing scallops to the lace.

Interfacing is rarely used with sheer or delicate laces, but is occasionally necessary for heavier opaque, underlined, or backed laces. If you intend to use interfacing make sure its weight is compatible with that of your lace.

For the beauty of the lace to stand on its own, make a separate camisole and underskirt of lining fabric. The lace can be attached at the waist, or may be handled as separate blouse and skirt units. Camisole, underskirt, or slip may be constructed of lining material or any stable fabric that works well with the lace. A separate slip dress of satin, taffeta, or tricot will combine modesty with intrigue when worn under a lacy caftan or flowing dress.

**Fabric Preparation:** Since net forms the background for most laces, you need not worry about grain. When straightening the ends of the fabric, concern yourself with the lace motifs. These may form a design that is horizontal or vertical, and cord may outline the motifs on the right side. Pre-shrink cotton and washable laces if necessary.

**Alterations and Fitting:** See page 11 for general information.

**Layouts:** Lace motifs should be advantageously placed whenever possible, to serve as decorative edges or trim on your garment.

If your lace is one which has a scalloped edge, pattern pieces can be positioned so that this forms a decorative finish along a straight neck edge or hemline. (To use the scallops along a curved edge, see page 23).

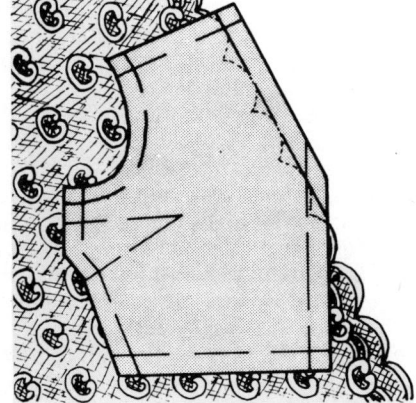

If your lace lacks a decorative edge, but has a motif which would make an attractive edge finish, you can lay out pattern pieces so an appropriate finished garment edge follows the motif. Cut around the motifs.

Make certain that you position each pattern piece correctly along the decorative edge of the lace; this should fall at either a seamline or a hemline in order to preserve original pattern dimensions. Cut with care.

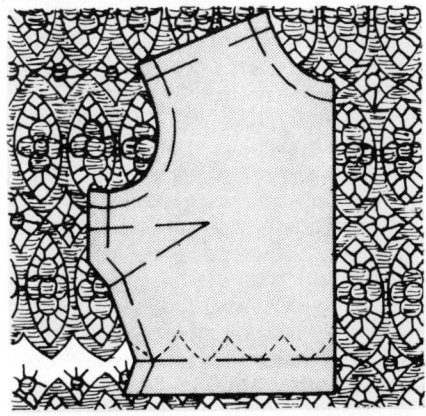

If you plan to appliqué the seams (see Construction, page 22), allow for the complete outline of the design on the front edges so these can be matched and lapped at the seamlines. You may want to emphasize the outline of the motif for easier cutting of intricate designs. With thread tracing, outline motif before cutting with contrasting thread.

**Marking:** Tailor's tacks work best; do not use a tracing wheel.

## Construction

Construction methods are determined by the sheerness or opacity, and delicacy of the lace, and by whether it is underlined, backed, or bonded. Fragile laces are handled as sheer fabrics while the others are constructed more conventionally.

**Pressing:** Use a press pad or Turkish towel under lace so the design will not be flattened by the iron.

and patted with your fingers—no iron on the fabric, please! A see-through press cloth is recommended, as it protects the fabric and prevents the iron from catching in the lace. Opaque laces can usually withstand steam-pressing if you use brown paper or a seam roll. Test first on fabric scraps.

**Seams and Darts:** Traditional methods of seam and dart construction may be employed on opaque or backed laces (pages 17-18). Structural seams in fragile laces are handled as for sheer fabrics; see pages 28-29 for construction details.

APPLIQUÉING THE SEAMS utilizes the concealing capacities of lace motifs. Plan the overlapping edges in your layout before cutting out pattern. Cut seams so the underlap seam allowance has a straight edge and the overlap seam allowance follows the lace motif. Match seamlines and pin so the edges overlap smoothly; baste From the outside, appliqué edge of motif to garment with tiny whipstitches or zigzag stitches(1). Trim away underlap seam allowance on the inside close to the stitches(2). A dart may be handled similarly by figuring its depth before overlapping.

ENCLOSED SEAMS are handled differently when maintaining the sheerness of lace is desirable. Self-fabric or net-faced edges are not interfaced, and a bound or appliquéd edge is strongly recommended. Substitute a binding of sheer net or organza, or appliqué a scalloped edge lace trim instead.

APPLIQUÉ LACE TRIM along an edge; adapt the lace you are using for the rest of the garment or use purchased lace trim. To make your own lace trim, cut along motifs to form an attractive strip. On the outside, place strip over garment with one edge along the seamline or hemline; pin and baste. Zigzag or whipstitch the remaining inner edge to the garment as explained in appliquéing the seam. Trim away excess garment fabric and press. For extremely curved edges, it may be necessary to make small clips between each motif, overlap the edges, and sew securely.

Opaque laces may be faced and interfaced as the fabric demands. Trim, clip, press, and favor the edge before understitching.

**Closures:** Underlined, backed, and medium to heavy opaque fabrics can usually support any closure. Zippers and buttonholes are restricted to opaque laces. In fine or lightweight laces, the weight of the closure may distort garment lines and destroy the fabric. Staystitch neckline ¾" from cut edge, trim away the ⅝" seam allowance, then bind the neckline with a sheer or satin fabric. Complete it with a tie, hook and eye, or snap closure — whichever is your preference.

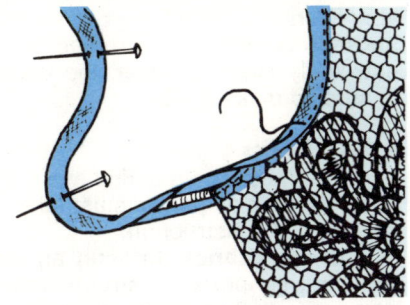

Some opaque laces lend themselves to buttonholes, but consider your fabric before proceeding. Be sure your fabric can withstand the handling involved with machine buttonholes. Loops and buttons are also a good closure.

**Hems:** Opaque, backed, or underlined laces may have hem edges finished in any of the traditional ways. On certain laces you can use a faced hem (page 37). Lace fabric with a scalloped edge can produce a lovely skirt or pants leg hem. A matching lace trim can be appliquéd on the edge.

NET FACING is an appropriate hem finish for many laces. For a 1" wide net hem, cut a strip of net 2½" wide. Fold strip in half lengthwise and baste it to the right side of the lace; extend raw edges ¼" beyond the hemline. Make two rows of medium length stitches, one row along the hemline, the other ⅛" from the first in the hem allowance; trim. Turn net in, favoring the garment edge at the hemline; slipstitch in place.

SCALLOPS along the edge of a shaped hem need planning. Fold fabric, matching scallops at edge. Place hemline along outer edge of scallop. To accommodate curve, cut lace along a motif and raise scallops by overlapping edges until correct shape is achieved; baste. Cut out skirt sections and hand or machine appliqué lace in its new position.

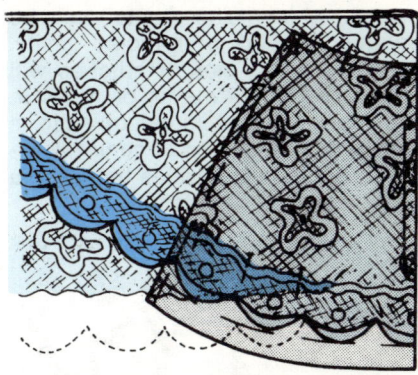

HORSEHAIR BRAID is another way to hem sheer laces. For construction details, see page 30.

**Care:** Follow instructions on hang-tag or end of bolt. Hang lace garments on padded hangers in garment bags for protection.

Tape hangers are a good addition to opaque or backed lace garments. Measure your garment from shoulder to a horizontal seamline. Cut ¼" satin ribbon four times your measurement minus 2". Cut ribbon into two equal lengths, overlap the ends of each ½", and stitch. Securely tack stitched ends to the seam allowances of horizontal seams.

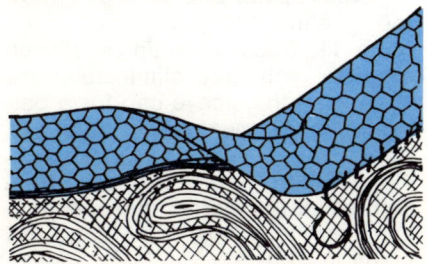

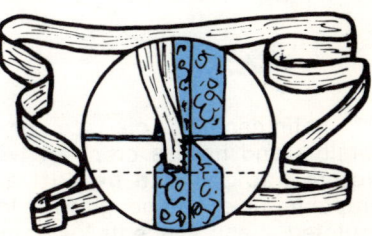

# Satin

The smoothness and luster of satin have made it a fashion favorite for years. Satin is woven in such a way that the lengthwise threads are caught by the crosswise threads after longer than usual intervals; this produces "floats" on the fabric surface which tend to reflect light and appear shiny. The floats can be snagged, soiled, or rumpled easily. Any misplaced pins or stitches will leave permanent marks or holes in the fabric. The shimmer of satin is highly desirable, but acquaint yourself with its peculiarities before you do any cutting or stitching.

Satin can be single-faced or reversible and have a crepe or twill-weave back. It can be soft and drapable, or crisp enough to hold a sculpted shape. Since its luster may seem to add to your visual dimensions, satin should be used wisely in your fashions. Whether your feeling for satin takes you into ruffles or an extremely elegant blazer, the fabric is sure to make a hit.

## Priorities

The facts about satin have a lot to do with the steps you must take to ready it for construction.

**Under Fabrics:** In satin an underlining supports construction and prevents stitches from showing on the outside. It helps eliminate pulled seams and the imprint of seam allowances on the right side after pressing. Use the lightest weight of underlining that will accomplish its purpose. Page 9 has fabric suggestions.

Interfacings and stiffenings may be eliminated if the fabric has enough body. They should be applied only to an underlined garment. Woven interfacings are recommended because they correspond to the construction of the satin.

Linings are often unnecessary. Let your pattern style and fabric weight be the determining factors.

**Fabric Preparation:** Fiber content is the best indication of the procedures to take for satin fabrics. Those made of cotton and polyester are nearly always washable and can be pre-shrunk by that method. Test a corner carefully, as some satins cannot even be steam-pressed; they water spot easily or may be dulled by steam-pressing (see page 25).

**Alterations and Fitting:** Follow the general fitting information on page 11. Because satin is difficult to ease, you may eliminate some ease from the sleeve cap for a better-fitting garment (see page 11). Allow wider seam allowances in close-fitting garments made from stiff satins to permit ease adjustment during fitting. Over-fitting will result in wrinkling.

**Layouts:** Since satin has a sheen, use a directional "With Nap" pattern layout. When positioning the pattern pieces, use fine silk pins only in the seam allowances—never in the garment area. To avoid snagging or over-handling, make sure your hands and finger nails are smooth and clean. If your hands are rough, try wearing lightweight cotton gloves when you work so the fabric won't be pulled or soiled.

**Marking:** The key thought here is to mark as little as possible. If you have used an underlining, all markings will be made on it. Baste the underlining to the satin in seam allowances only. Use clean, white or pastel thread.

## Construction

Throughout construction, satin should be handled as little as possible. From first seam to final hem, keep the fabric surface in its original un-marred state.

**Pressing:** Take all of the precautions discussed in fabric preparation here as well. Use a warm, dry iron and a gentle, light touch for most satins as steam may cause permanent puckers or dulled fibers. Make sure the sole plate of your iron is smooth and free of discolorations. Use a press cloth or tissue paper for extra protection—even when pressing from the wrong side, the slightest pressure from the iron may be enough to mar some satins. Seams may be opened with only finger-pressing for a soft look (see page 37 for this method).

In delicate satins, press each seam open over a seam roll, or with brown paper under the seam allowances to protect the fabric. (You may be able to press the seams without this equipment if your fabric is not one which mars easily.) Pre-test as follows on a sample seam: first press the seam open (1), then use the side of the iron to press beneath the seam allowances and smooth out any ridges (2).

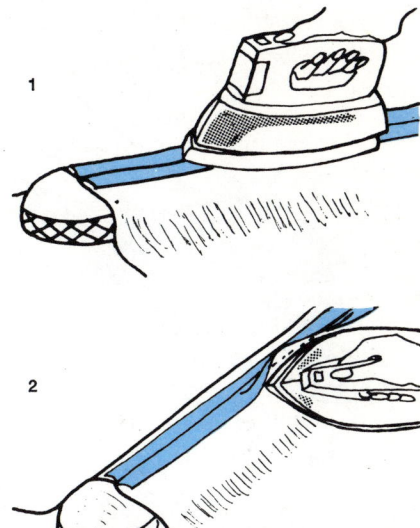

The degree of pressure you use will determine the finished appearance of garment edges. A lighter touch will give the softer roll needed for hems, while a more firm touch will make collars and cuffs take a crisp edge. Do not over-press.

**Seams:** Testing seaming procedures in satin is a must. Use approximately 14-16 stitches to the inch, and hold the fabric taut as you stitch to prevent its creeping or puckering. Also prevent puckered seams by using silk or polyester thread. Use a seam finish for structural seams that ravel considerably. Refer to pages 17-18 for stitched and overcast, machine zigzag, and bound seam finishes. For a more elegant touch, use the HONG KONG FINISH: cut 1" wide bias strips of underlining or lightweight fabric, joining as needed to make a continuous strip. With right sides together, match one edge of bias strip with cut edge of seam allowance. Stitch bias to garment in a ¼" seam, keeping the garment free. Turn bias to inside over the seam, encasing the raw edge; press. From the right side of the seam allowance, stitch in the seam, catching free edge of binding.

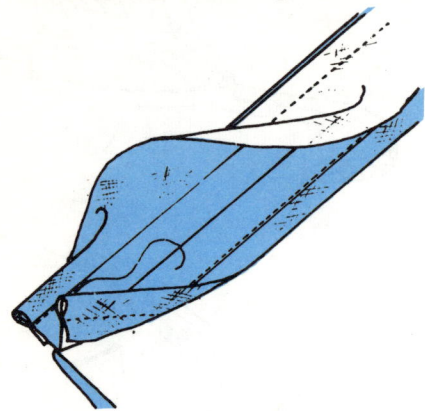

Enclosed seams will require understitching (page 15) if there is any possibility of their rolling and showing from the outside.

**Closures:** In delicate satin garments, the weight of a zipper or buttons may distort the closure area. Use an invisible zipper or a hand-sewn regular zipper for the best finish. Almost any type of buttonhole or decorative closure can be used if applied properly. Buttons that are jeweled or have rough edges may catch and pull fabric floats. Sew these buttons on garment overlap and fasten garment edges with a snap sewn to the underlap and the underside of the overlap.

**Hems:** You may use any of the recommended seam finishes plus ribbon or bias seam binding, or lace as a hem finish. If the hem needs support and shaping, use the interfaced hem (see page 18).

For a softly rolled PADDED HEM, use an interfaced hem with either lamb's wool, flannel strips, or soft cable cord. Cut a 1" wide strip of padding and position it so ⅓ of the strip is below the hemline and ⅔, above it. Sew padding to interfacing at the hemline with long running stitches (not shown). Or, place cable cord along the hemline for padding and sew to interfacing with long loose catchstitches. Complete the hem.

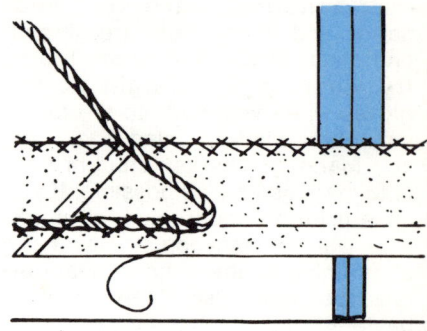

If the hem is curved, it may be difficult to finish unless some of the excess fabric is removed first. Refer to the hemming procedures on pages 33-34 for two ways of resolving the situation.

**Care:** After your garment has been completed, you'll want to care for it in the best possible way. Hang your garment on a padded hanger to support the shoulder area. If the skirt is heavy, add tape hangers at the waistline (see page 23). Stuff tissue paper into the sleeves and bodice to keep these areas smooth and wrinkle-free.

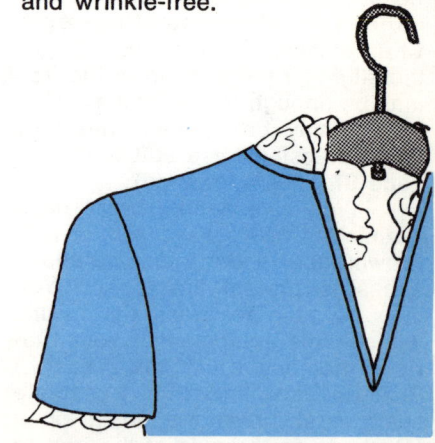

# Seductive Selection

Both sheers and crepes tell all, and require as much love and attention as you can afford them. Sheers can be filmy, clinging, and soft, or clear and crisp. Sheerness comes in varying degrees, and construction details will be visible in most of these fabrics. Crepe is a fluid fabric —soft and body-hugging by nature— and is made in many weights of many different fibers. Every ridge, bulge, and curve you have will be revealed by crepe, so consider your choice of style and undergarments carefully. Sewing these fabrics correctly will ensure that yours will be a beautiful garment.

## Sheers

Sheer refers to a general fabric characteristic, rather than any particular fabric. Sheer fabrics can be knitted or woven in any color. Novelty sheers may have metallic threads, embroidered motifs, and burn-out, flocked, or printed designs. Fiber content—cotton, silk, wool, or man-made fibers — determines the specific nature of each sheer fabric —soft, crisp, supple, or firm. Soft sheers have an airy, drapable texture. Organza, batiste, and georgette provide fluid lines of their own, while transparent chiffon and tricot cling to your body's lines. Crisp sheers have a firmness determined by weave, finish, and fiber that makes them easier to handle than their soft counterparts. Voile, organdy, dimity, marquisette, and net, along with translucent fabrics like dotted Swiss are sheers with varying degrees of crispness. Other crisp sheers may be decorated with embroidery or flocked designs.

An appropriate fabric weight should be evaluated on the basis of the garment for which it will be used, as well as the time of day in which it will be worn. Remember, sheers can be very revealing. Use the qualities of sheers to your best advantage.

## Priorities

Sheers—especially those which are soft—require maximum care in handling. By employing the special techniques we have outlined in this section, you can achieve flawlessly constructed seams.

**Under Fabrics:** If your pattern and design call for the use of under fabrics, be certain that your choice is compatible in fiber and care with the sheer you plan to use. You may want to underline a dress, limiting the see-through effect of your fabric to the sleeves only. An underlining makes a more durable garment, and provides modesty as well.

Underlined garments may require interfacing, but be careful when matching the weight of it to your fashion fabric. Try to eliminate the use of interfacing entirely, or substitute self- or underlining fabric for extra support. Often, eliminating facings results in a lovelier garment—to do this, bind the edges with self- or contrasting fabric.

A traditionally applied lining is not used on sheers unless your garment is completely underlined. Camisoles, under-dresses, and underskirts are familiar companions to sheer garments. They may be constructed of lining or another glamorous fabric compatible with your sheer fabric.

**Fabric Preparation:** Straighten fabric ends and pre-shrink washable sheers as instructed on page 10.

**Alterations and Fitting:** In soft sheers, make all your pattern alterations and test in a very soft muslin before cutting your fashion fabric. Crisp sheers are less delicate, and do not usually present problems. See page 11 for fitting information. Do not over-fit—the fabric may be too fragile to withstand even a small amount of strain on the seams.

**Layouts:** See pages 11-12 for general information on cutting layouts. To prevent slippage and to make layout easier, chiffon and other filmy fabrics should be secured to the cutting board or to a sheet secured to the table. Check your fabric to determine whether a "With Nap" layout is necessary. Sharp needles can be used to pin pattern to the fabric.

**Marking:** Some opaque sheers can be marked with a tracing wheel and paper; test a fabric scrap to see whether markings show. If you underline your sheer, mark underlining fabric. Transparent sheers must be marked carefully—be sure your marking is not permanent. Pins and chalk are best.

## Construction

When handling sheers, remember that construction details are visible—take a little more time to produce flawless seams, closures, and hems.

**Pressing:** Test heat and pressure on scraps of your sheer fabric. Use steam with discretion as it may cause some fibers to pucker permanently. Press enclosed seams as for lace (pages 21-22).

**Seams:** Chiffon, georgette, and organza are difficult to stitch because the crosswise yarns do not always stay perpendicular to the lengthwise yarns when handled. Stitch seams with the help of tissue paper (see page 15) on one or both sides of your seams. A sheer that has not been underlined requires finished seams.

Opaque or underlined sheers can employ a variety of structural and enclosed seams. Seams that work well with sheer fabrics are the FRENCH SEAM, FRENCH WHIPPED SEAM with an overcast or zigzag finish, SIMULATED FRENCH SEAM, and the SELF-BOUND SEAM — all are illustrated on these pages.

FRENCH SEAM

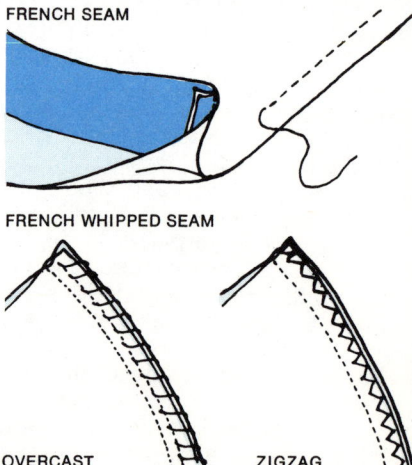

FRENCH WHIPPED SEAM

OVERCAST      ZIGZAG

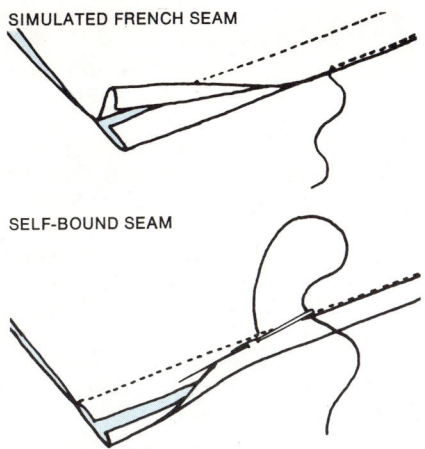

SIMULATED FRENCH SEAM

SELF-BOUND SEAM

Enclosed seams for sheers without underlining or interfacing should be trimmed to 1/8".

**Closures:** Choose closures with great care. The weight of zippers and buttons may distort lightweight sheer fabrics, but these may be perfect closures for underlined sheers. For slightly or loosely fitted garments, use a continuous lap opening with snaps, or hooks and thread eyes (1). Refer to The Vogue Sewing Book if you need construction advice.

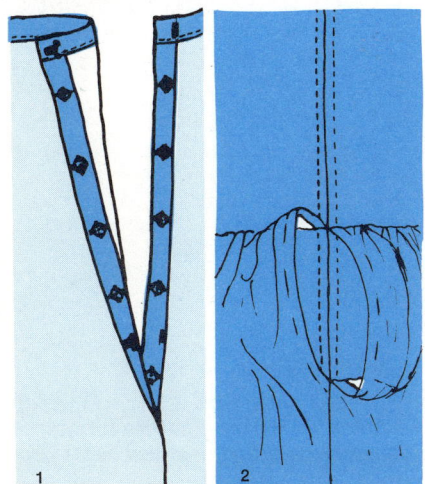

For a garment with an underlined bodice (2, above), and an underskirt with a sheer overskirt, plan zipper opening carefully. Finish the opening edges of the sheer overskirt by turning the edges in along seamline and narrow hemming them. Match these edges to the seamline of the underskirt. Sew zipper to bodice by hand or machine, ending at waist seam. Then sew zipper to underskirt only, keeping finished edges of overskirt free.

**Hems:** For an underlined garment, use a plain hem. Sheer skirts that are not shaped may have hems from 3"-10" deep, depending on your fabric. Turn in the raw edge 1/4" to finish hem edge; slipstitch.

For curved hems, you have several finishes from which to choose. A HAND ROLLED HEM is suggested for curved or straight hems in soft, chiffon-type sheers. Machine stitch 1/4" from raw edge; trim. Roll the fabric between thumb and forefinger about 1/8"; slipstitch with single stitches.

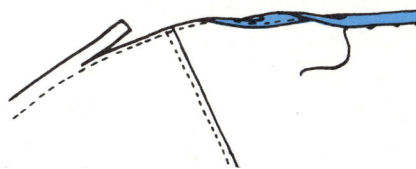

A MACHINE HEM for sheers combines cording and zigzag stitching. Use a special purpose presser foot and your sewing machine manual for instructions.

A NARROW HEM lends itself to curved hems. Plan a 3/8" hem allowance. Turn raw edge in 3/16" and then another 3/16" to encase edge. Sew in place by hand or machine.

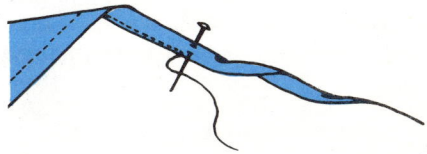

For sheer hems that need more body without adding weight, use horsehair braid or a thin wire for stiffening. Carefully mark the hemline with basting stitches. Begin a NARROW HORSEHAIR BRAID HEM by steam-pressing braid to eliminate creases. Cut braid to fit hem circumference plus ¾" for lapping ends; see page 35 for finishing ends. Trim hem allowance to ½". Pin braid to the right side of the fabric with edges even; stitch ¼" from edges (1). Turn braid inside along hemline and baste close to fold (2). Secure remaining edge of braid.

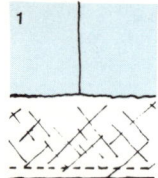 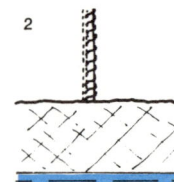

To make a WIRE HEM, use a thin, flexible wire or cloth-covered millinery wire. Finish wire ends by overlapping them and wrapping them with thread. Plan a 1" hem allowance for easier handling. Place wire on the inside along hemline. Encase wire in hem allowance and zigzag in place with small stitches. Trim hem allowance to stitching.

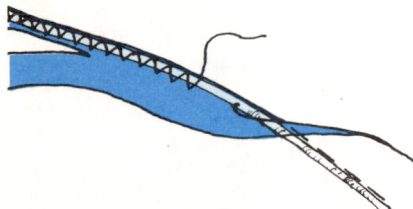

**Care:** Soft sheers require tender care. They can be treated much the same as velvets, except that shower steaming might do damage to some, like chiffon and georgette. Washable crisp or soft sheers should be cleaned according to instructions on fabric bolt.

# Crepe

Crepe fabrics have a pebbly or crinkled surface created by crimped fibers, twisted yarns, fabric construction, or finishing process. Crepe can be knitted or woven of almost any fiber. Weight is determined by fiber and fabric construction. Use light- to medium weight crepes for flowing designs, and save the heavier weights for more structured garments. The clinging qualities of crepe may work for or against you—every curve, bulge, and strap will show in fitted garments.

## Priorities

The structure of crepe fabrics makes them difficult to handle as you sew. Satin-back and plain crepe have a tendency to slip and slide. Use the following methods to make sewing these fabrics easy.

**Under Fabrics:** The most important consideration when using under fabrics is to match their fiber and care properties with those of your crepe. The use of underlining is rarely necessary, but when your design does require it, choose a soft, lightweight batiste or organza.

Interfacing should be soft and lightweight, and relate directly to the weight of your fabric. Never use interfacing to stiffen—it should add only body and support. Batiste and permanent press interfacing fabrics are suggested. When you have underlined a crepe garment, you may eliminate the use of interfacing entirely or use a second layer of underlining fabric. Never use a fusible interfacing or adhesive on crepes.

Lining is not used in its traditional form in crepe garments unless your fabric is of a heavy weight. Sometimes garment type dictates the need for a lining—a soft wool crepe blazer or jacket may require a lining. Lining fabric may also be used to make a camisole top to support a full skirt.

**Fabric Preparation:** See page 10 for general information.

**Alterations and Fitting:** Follow the general information given on page 11. Never over-fit your crepe garment as it will wrinkle and creep unattractively on the body.

**Layouts:** See page 11 when preparing your pattern layout, giving special attention to shading; some crepes are directional. To avoid pulls or snagging, cover your cutting surface with a sheet which has been securely anchored.

**Marking:** Pins and chalk are suggested, but see page 12 for more methods. Test before using.

## Construction

Lightweight and slippery crepes require that garment sections be positioned and seams be basted with silk or cotton-wrapped polyester thread.

**Pressing:** Test-press on fabric scraps before pressing. Some crepes are shrunk by steam, while others are puckered—test a dry iron on scraps to determine the heat setting. Use a press cloth and do not over-press, as this flattens the texture.

**Seams:** Use tissue paper strips under the seams when sewing on the machine; be careful not to stretch seams as you stitch. Tape may be needed to stay some crepes at shoulders and other points of strain; enclosed seams like cutaway armholes may need tape, too (see page 15). Otherwise, enclosed and structural seams are handled in the traditional manner.

**Closures:** Refer to the sheer fabrics section, page 29, for closures that can be applied to crepes as well. A zipper may be used if its weight can be supported by the fabric. Either an invisible zipper or a hand-picked application of a regular zipper will make a fine closure. The type of buttonhole suitable for crepe depends on the ability of your fabric to withstand the handling involved. Machine buttonholes should be carefully made with the help of tissue paper. Be certain that your fabric can withstand the extra stitching before making machine buttonholes.

**Hems:** Hang garment overnight before marking hem. You will find appropriate hemming techniques in the sections on velvets, satins, and sheers — choose the best method for your garment.

**Care:** Check the hang-tag or the end of the bolt for cleaning instructions. Most crepe garments can be hung in your closet, but some bias-cut styles may need to be folded with tissue paper and stored flat. Use tape hangers (page 23) to help support your garment.

# The Elegant Ones

Let your more adventurous side rule, and include one or all of these fabrics in your wardrobe for those special occasions. Select what suits your mood—feminine taffeta, elegant brocade, bright-light metallics, or opulent beaded fabrics — then make it very personally yours.

## Taffeta

The crisp rustle of taffeta brings to mind a vision of hoop skirts in a turn-of-the-century parlor. Its current appeal takes almost any form from shirtdresses or pleated skirts to leg-of-mutton sleeves and ruffles. It's also a favorite for slips, camisoles, and accompaniments to sheer or lace creations. Its crispness gives taffeta beauty, but may cause construction problems.

The most familiar taffeta is a fine plain weave fabric and is usually of a man-made fiber. It has a lustrous appearance and crisp hand, and it can be found in a variety of forms. Taffeta may also be made of natural fibers and have a mat finish and soft hand. Faille taffeta has fine ribs while paper taffeta is lightweight and has a crisp paper-like finish. Changeable taffeta is so called because two different colors are used in the warp and filling, giving it an iridescent surface. Tissue taffeta is lightweight and transparent, yet still has crispness. Moiré is classified as a taffeta since it shares the same general properties. In finishing, it is pressed by heated rollers to produce a watered surface appearance.

The luster of taffeta makes its fashion use important: a light color or a shiny surface visually adds pounds, while a darker, dull surface minimizes a fuller figure.

Save heavier taffeta or moirés for sculptured shapes; use the lighter tissue or paper taffetas for delicate silhouettes.

## Priorities

These planning and preparation tips will help make your taffeta garment a complete success.

**Under Fabrics:** Traditional underlining is not always necessary; its main advantage is for marking. Since taffeta has a tendency to crack rather than gently bend when folded, all garment folds or creases need the support of interfacing. Add stiffening agents when your design requires some extra support to keep its shape. Your choice of a lining will be dependent on the garment style. When using lining in a traditional method, refer to construction tips and techniques offered in The Vogue Sewing Book.

**Fabric Preparation:** Since taffeta is handled like satin, refer to that section and page 10.

**Alterations and Fitting:** Review page 11 for general information. Allow 1" seam allowances for extra ease in fitting. Do not over-fit as fabric may crack and wrinkle.

**Layouts:** General layout information is on pages 11-12. To avoid unnecessary marks, place pins in seam allowances only.

**Marking:** See page 12 for general marking methods. Test and use one that does not leave permanent marks.

## Construction

Learning a few sewing tips can do no harm when working with taffeta.

**Pressing:** Since taffeta has a sheen and mars easily, it reacts to pressing much as satin would. Refer to the suggestions on page 25.

**Seams:** Machine stitching and seaming techniques are on pages 14-15. The special applications for satin (pages 25-26) apply here, too. Taffeta has a tendency to ravel; finish seams with the stitched and overcast (page 17), zigzag (page 18), or Hong Kong (pages 25-26) finish.

**Supporting Ruffle:** One popular stiffener for gathered skirts is a supporting ruffle. Cut a strip of organdy or other suitable stiffening fabric twice the desired width and the same circumference as the skirt section before gathering. Fold strip in half lengthwise and turn in the narrow ends ⅝" and stitch. Gather raw edges, and adjust to the finished circumference. Pin to waist seam allowances only, distributing gathers evenly, and place finished ends so they won't catch in zipper or interfere with closure. Stitch to seam allowance only, using two rows of stitching; or, bind gathered edge and sew securely for easy removal.

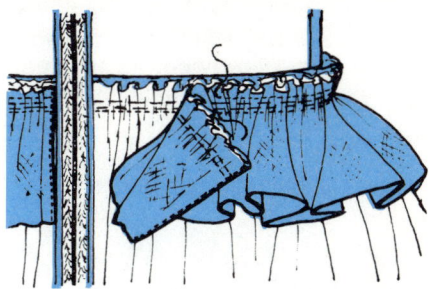

**Closures:** Insert a regular zipper by hand or use an invisible one. Buttonholes can be made by any of the standard methods. Jeweled buttons may pull fabric threads; see page 26 for alternate suggestions.

**Hems:** To keep taffeta from forming a flat crease at the hem, use an interfaced hem (page 18) or padded hem (page 26).

Curved taffeta hems need special easing attention. To handle fullness in a slightly curved hem, restitch seam below the hemline at a slant opposite that of garment above hemline.

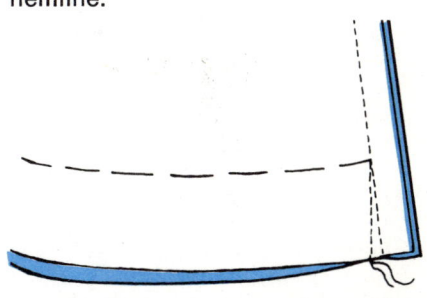

Remove previous stitching and trim seam below hemline to ¼"; complete with appropriate finish.

For extremely curved hems or those which are shaped so hem edge and garment circumferences do not correspond, another method may be used. At evenly spaced intervals, slash the hem allowance no deeper than 1" from the fold. Keep the garment free as you are working with hem area. To eliminate excess fabric, cut narrow wedges along slashes, bring the cut edges together, and hemstitch. To add width to the hem allowance, insert small wedges of fabric and hemstitch.

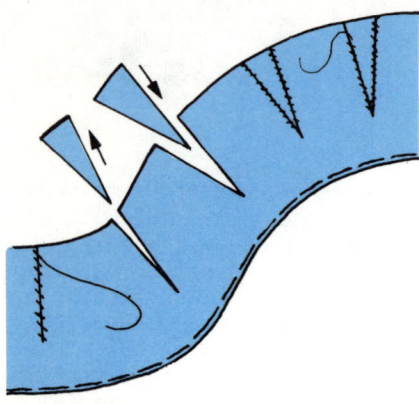

If your taffeta fabric ravels extensively, try using a faced hem (see page 37).

**Care:** The care you'd give a taffeta garment is much the same as you would give a garment made of velvet or satin. It should be placed where nothing will rub against it, since taffeta is easily abraded. To help the garment keep its shape between wearings, stuff sleeves, bust area, and flared or gathered skirts with tissue paper (see page 26). Always hang taffeta garments on padded hangers so the shoulder line will not crack and form unsightly ridges. Dry clean garment or care for it as recommended by fabric manufacturer.

# Brocade

Rich, opulent brocade may be traditionally floral in design or have contemporary motifs. The interwoven design is flat or raised, and completely covers the fabric. Brocades are reversible fabrics — thus you may have two choices of design in the same fabric. Choose your favorite side and be consistent with your choice, or consider using one side of the fabric for the major portion of your garment and the other side for a contrasting portion. Other similar fabrics include piqué, brocatelle, matelassé, and jacquard knits. Note fiber content carefully; whenever brocades contain metal threads, handle them like metallics.

Let fabric weight, drapability, and density guide your pattern choice. Flat designs may add no visual bulk unless the fibers are lustrous; raised designs add dimension and must be used carefully.

## Priorities

Brocades with flat or raised designs, fillers, and metallic threads require some thought when preparing the fabric for your garment.

**Under Fabrics:** Brocades share qualities with satin and taffeta; refer to those sections for suggestions.

**Fabric Preparation:** General methods are given on page 10. Some brocades may be steam-pressed, others will mar.

**Alterations and Fitting:** Refer to page 11 for general tips. Fitting brocades may require the removal of excess ease from the sleeve cap (see page 11).

**Layouts:** Always use a "With Nap" layout as brocades may be directional or shaded. Large design motifs may require matching. Plan your layout with care, using the sides of the fabric consistently. Pin only in seam allowances to avoid pulled threads.

**Marking:** A tracing wheel may cut design threads, so test first. Tailor's chalk is good for most flat or slightly raised brocades; tailor's tacks are best for raised designs.

## Construction

From start to finish, incorporate the following information in every garment construction step.

**Pressing:** When pressing seams for raised brocades, pad your ironing board with a towel so fabric surface will not be flattened. Protect loose design threads with a press cloth. Pages 21-22 have additional pressing tips for textured fabrics.

**Seams:** Refer to pages 14-15 for general information. Hold fabric taut as you stitch to prevent puckers. If brocade ravels, use the stitched and overcast (page 17), machine zig-zag (page 18), bound (page 18), or Hong Kong (pages 25-26) finish.

**Closures:** Fabric weight and design dimension influence closure choice. Machine or hand-worked buttonholes are good for all brocades. Restrict the use of zippers—either invisible or a hand-sewn regular type—to brocades having flat designs and few metallic threads (these might break when creased). Bound buttonholes may be difficult to make in brocades that ravel or are thick. See page 26 for how to use jeweled buttons and other closures.

**Hems:** If your brocade needs support in the hem area, use an interfaced hem (page 18) or a padded hem (page 26). For curved hems, refer to pages 33-34.

For an extra-stiff hem, apply WIDE HORSEHAIR BRAID in an underlined brocade. Steam creases from braid; cut it to fit hem plus ¾". Lap ends ¾", and enclose them in a fabric strip applied with two rows of edgestitching. Easestitch along one braid edge if not pre-threaded. Place unthreaded edge along hemline with enclosed ends of braid over a seam; baste. Check hemline, then sew basted edge of braid to underlining with long hemming stitches. Draw up ease thread at upper braid edge to control fullness; sew to underlining with long running stitches before completing.

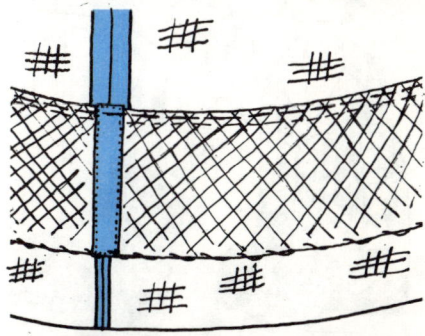

**Care:** Generally, you are advised to hang garments on padded hangers and store them in an uncrowded area of your closet. Stuff clothes with tissue (page 26) if needed. Most brocade fabrics and their relatives should be dry cleaned, but some piqués and jacquard knits may be machine washable and dryable. Read hang-tags or end of fabric bolt for care requirements.

# Metallics

Glittering metallic fabrics have a radiance that is sure to steal the scene. From dazzling lamés to delicate Benares to iridescent brocades, any fabric that contains some metal threads is called a metallic. Knitted or woven, metallics can range from soft sheers to crisp, heavily textured fabrics. These special fabrics deserve the very best of care, too, because many metal fibers are tarnished or discolored by steam.

Use metallics with a liberal fashion sense. Sheer Benares is perfect for a soft, draped look, while a stretch metallic knit would make a slinky jumpsuit. Even heavily designed metallic brocades have a use in theater suits or evening coats and capes. Remember that fabric density and light reflection will visually affect body dimension.

## Priorities

Handle metallics gently to prepare for construction.

**Under Fabrics:** Underlining is not always necessary, but may be desirable to keep metallic threads from breaking at seams. Base your decision upon fiber and fabric weight. For interfacing information refer to page 9. Lining is a necessity if metallic threads will scratch or irritate skin; use a soft, dense fabric for this. To further prevent skin irritation, add satin cording to such garment edges as necklines, armholes, and hems.

**Fabric Preparation:** See page 10 for general information. Test to see if steam pressing will tarnish or discolor metal threads. Creases in fabric may be permanent, since metallic threads break easily.

**Alterations and Fitting:** Pattern alteration and fitting tips are on page 11. Cut wider seam allowances to ensure ease for vertical fitting. Remove excess ease from sleeve caps in fabrics that are heavy or resist shrinking.

**Layouts:** Pages 11-12 provide basic information on layouts. Use a "With Nap" layout for metallic fabrics because of their directional light reflection. Place pins only in seam allowances; avoid placing pattern pieces on permanent creases. Use expendable shears to cut metallics, since blades will become dull.

**Marking:** A tracing wheel and dressmaker's tracing paper are best left for other fabrics, since they may cut metallic threads. Use carefully placed tailor's tacks.

## Construction

Stitching your metallic fabric requires careful consideration of the desired results.

**Pressing:** Because steam will often tarnish or discolor metal threads, test pressing techniques.

The pressure of the iron may cause metal threads to break, exposing rough ends. Protecting your fabric by wearing a thimble, finger-press seams open or edges in place.

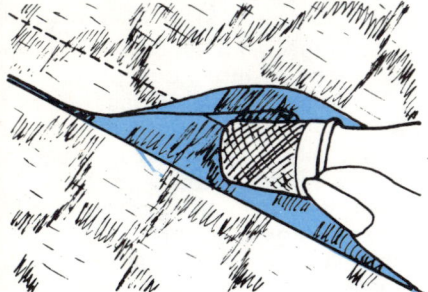

**Seams:** Metallic fabrics may be permanently marked by a misplaced seam. Use fine needles and synthetic thread for construction. Change machine needles as they become too dull to stitch correctly. It may be necessary to stitch the seam with tissue paper (page 15). If fabric is heavy, tape seams (page 15) for support. Test your seaming techniques before construction.

Use satin piping to make a garment edge that will not scratch. Baste piping to garment along seamline. Lap ends as shown when there is no garment opening; remove any filler where the ends cross. Or, extend ends into seam allowances at opening edges. Baste facing or full lining over cording; stitch, using a zipper foot. When facing or lining is turned to inside, the finished edge is smooth.

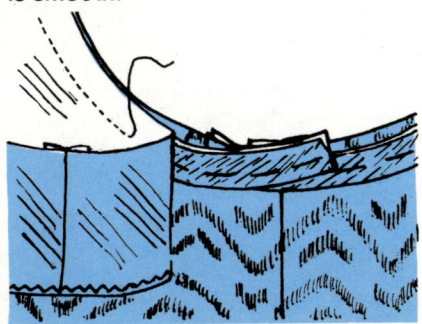

**Closures:** Base closure decisions on fabric weight, density, and the size and flexibility of metal threads. Save regular and invisible zippers for flexible metallics that won't break when creased. You can use buttonholes and buttons for most metallics, but restrict bound ones to fabrics which do not ravel. See page 26 for other closures.

**Hems:** A standard hem may be used if metallic thread is non-irritating or is covered by lining. Use the interfaced hem (page 18) or padded hem (page 26) for additional support.

To provide a smooth finish or to protect hose from snagging, use the FACED HEM. For facing, cut a 2" wide bias strip of lining fabric; or, use commercial bias hem facing. Shape bias to match curve of hem at hemline. Lap right side of facing ¼" over marked hemline and stitch in a ¼" seam; turn in facing ends ¼" to meet. Trim away excess hem allowance and turn facing to inside along hemline. Turn in raw facing edge ¼" and sew to garment; sew facing ends together.

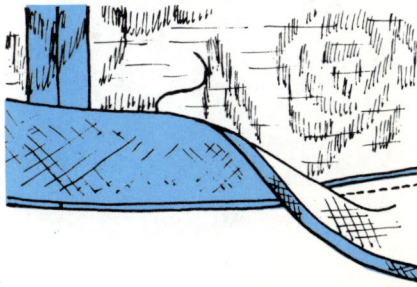

If desired, include satin piping for a piped hem edge.

**Care:** A metallic garment is best stored on a padded hanger in your closet; do not fold it. Ribbon hangers (page 23) sewn into the garment may be needed for extra support. Fill out garment curves with tissue paper to keep metal threads from being broken. Clean as recommended on hang-tag or bolt end.

# Beaded Fabrics

Beaded fabrics exist in many forms. One of these is sure to be perfect for almost any occasion. Beads, sequins, and rhinestones may be sewn individually, with a continuous thread, or secured with metal prongs. Applied to a base fabric that may be knitted or woven, they may be encrusted in a general all-over design or sprinkled in random motifs.

Both the base fabric and the surface details are your guides to construction and care. Consider fabric density and visual effect when planning a beaded fashion. The heaviness of some beaded fabrics may make them impractical for your fashion goals. Elaborately encrusted fabrics will be most attractive when made in simple designs. Whether you plan on a beaded evening dress, a sequinned pants top, or just a rhinestone-covered collar and lapels, it's sure to be a fashion bauble worth making.

## Priorities

Beaded fabrics are a challenge; these procedures will make it one that is fun to accept.

**Under Fabrics:** Pages 9-10 contain information on under fabrics. An underlining or backing is essential to cover the threads and prongs used to attach beads; use a soft, dense fabric. Interfacing, when used, follows standard methods. Lining is desirable. Cut facings of lining fabric or of your fashion fabric after removing the beads; do not mar the base fabric. Satin piping (page 37) at finished edges will prevent skin irritation.

**Fabric Preparation:** Refer to page 10 for information. When some beads, sequins, or rhinestones are washed, their finish disappears or their metal prongs rust. Steam-pressing may dull or damage beads and sequins, too. See the pressing tips on the next page.

**Alterations and Fitting:** All of the pattern alterations and fitting techniques on page 11 apply here.

**Layouts:** Always use a "With Nap" layout. If individual motifs are large, position them attractively on finished garment; match motifs if necessary for continuity. Pin only in seam allowances to avoid pulled threads or broken beads. Use expendable shears for cutting. When beads fall on the cutting line, cut outside of them to maintain an ample seam allowance width.

When beads or sequins are extremely close, you may have to use small scissors to clip them from the fabric along the cutting line before cutting through the base fabric. Cut a heavily encrusted fabric one layer at a time. If you are working with a loosely knitted or woven fabric that is beaded, staystitch the seam allowances immediately after cutting to prevent losing beads.

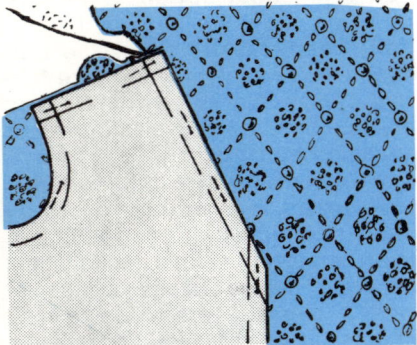

**Marking:** The basic marking methods are listed on page 12. The clearest method is tailor's tacks. Use a slightly contrasting color. Tracing wheel and paper should be avoided at all costs. Tailor's chalk may work if there are not too many loose threads on the wrong side of fabric.

## Construction

Further your knowledge of fabric handling with these special hints.

**Pressing:** In construction, as in fabric preparation, press with low heat. Avoid steam since it may discolor or ruin beads. Pad the ironing board with a thick towel, and using a press cloth, press the wrong side of the fabric. It may be advisable to finger-press seams (pages 36-37).

**Seams:** Accuracy is important since beads must be removed from seam allowances before stitching. Pin or hand baste garment sections together, and fit before stitching. Baste darts from outside of garment to fit them.

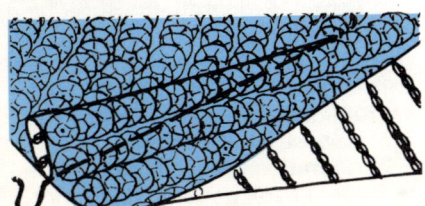

To baste seams, lap one garment section over the other, matching seamlines. Pin or baste for fitting; use diagonal basting for seams in heavily beaded fabrics.

After fitting, mark new seamlines and dart lines. Remove beads to the marking from dart area and seam allowances. Fasten bead threads by hand or sew them in the seam; save the removed beads for later use. Baste securely to prevent slippage; stitch seams and darts, using a zipper or cording foot. When a beaded fabric is sewn to another fabric, follow the same procedure. Replace all missing or broken beads along seamlines after completion.

**Closures:** Remove beads from seam allowances before installing a zipper. Buttonholes are impractical on fully beaded fabrics—substitute decorative fasteners and clips, or make a continuous lap cut from lining fabric (page 29).

**Hems:** Remove beads from hem allowance. For support, use the interfaced hem (page 18), padded hem (page 26), or wide horsehair braid hem (page 35). For heavily beaded fabrics or curved hems, use a faced hem (page 37).

**Care:** Tape hangers (page 23) are needed if the fabric is heavy. Use padded hangers to prevent the shoulders from creasing. Save beads removed during construction for touch-up jobs. Clean the garment by the method that is best for both base fabric and beads.

# Knit Specialties

As times and lifestyles change, jerseys and stretch knits have established themselves as modern classics. Jerseys, whether matte, napped, or with metallic threads, fit into our everyday and special occasions with easy-going comfort.

JERSEY

STRETCHY KNIT

## Jerseys

Jerseys may be stable or have moderate stretch. They are available in many weights, textures, colors, and fibers. They may stretch both lengthwise and crosswise or crosswise only—this facilitates achieving a body-hugging silhouette. Jerseys do not require special patterns as some knit fabrics do, but they require special treatment in preparation and construction to ensure retention of the flexibility of the fabric. Fiber content dictates the procedures to be taken with these fabrics. Jerseys are soft by nature, and must be handled carefully to prevent snagging and running.

Select fabric weight according to your pattern needs—a clingy dress or jumpsuit design requires a light, supple jersey; a jacket, suit, or cape design needs a heavier weight. Jerseys are clinging and should be used to your advantage.

### Priorities

Remember that you are dealing with a fabric that may stretch.

**Under Fabrics:** If you intend to use under fabrics, match their fiber and care factors precisely to those of your fabric. Underlining may inhibit softness and clinging, but it may be necessary to make an open or loose knit appear more opaque, or to prevent stretching your knit out of shape. To underline a jersey that is not stable, see Vogue Patterns' "Everything About Sewing Knits."

Use interfacing with heavier jerseys if necessary, but limit its use to small areas. A better idea may be to substitute a layer of self-fabric, rather than a traditional interfacing, for the support you desire.

Lining is rarely needed except for heavier jersey jackets, coats, and capes. To keep certain garments properly positioned on your body you may want to add an inside belt as described on page 19.

**Fabric Preparation:** Straighten grain if the wale (lengthwise grain) and course (crosswise grain) are not correctly aligned. See page 10 for instructions. Pre-shrink your fabric if it is wash-and-wear.

**Alterations and Fitting:** Refer to page 11 for general information.

Jerseys may require more extensive fitting after your pattern has been cut out.

**Layout:** Because most knits tend to have directional shading, use a "With Nap" layout (page 11). Cut carefully, leaving 1" seam allowances if you anticipate slight circumference fitting adjustments. Use ball point or silk pins to prevent snagging and consequential running. Use only very sharp shears for cutting jerseys.

**Marking:** Because tracing wheels can damage jerseys, pins and chalk or tailor's tacks are recommended.

## Construction

Construction techniques for jerseys are those which apply to all stretch knits. On fabric scraps, test all unfamiliar methods.

**Pressing:** Too much pressure on the iron may cause seam allowance imprints to show on right side of fabric. Use brown paper under seam allowances, or press lightly along seamline under each seam allowance (page 25). Do not over-press jerseys; use steam with caution.

**Seams:** Hold seams taut while stitching, but do not stretch them. Use thread with "give" properties— cotton-wrapped polyester is a wise choice. Tissue paper helps in stitching stretchy seams (see page 15). Tape shoulders and curves (like a neck or sleeveless armhole) to prevent stretching (page 15).

Structural seams can be stitched and finished with two rows of zigzag stitching ¼" apart. Trim away the excess seam allowance.

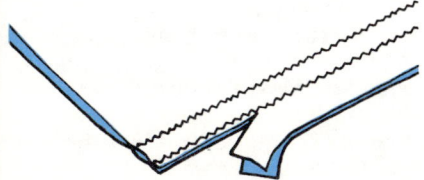

Edgestitch seam allowances, facings, and hem edges to prevent their rolling.

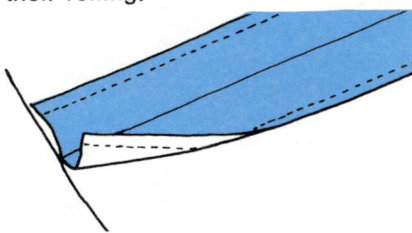

**Closures:** Refer to sheers (page 29) for closures suitable for jerseys.

**Hems:** Heavier jerseys may require more than one row of stitches to support the hem. If so, use a DOUBLE CATCHSTITCHED HEM.

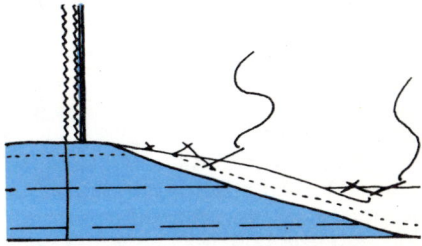

**Care:** Depending on the weight of the fabric, either hang your finished garment on a padded hanger or fold and store it flat. If the fabric is washable, follow instructions on hang-tag or end of bolt.

## Super-Stretchables

Complete information on construction techniques for stretchy knits can be found in "Everything About Sewing Swimwear" and "Everything About Sewing Knits." Only those patterns specified as suitable for "two-way stretch knits" or "stretchable unbonded knits" should be used with these flexible fabrics. Body-clinging garments are your goal, whether your fabric is plain, ribbed, or textured. From tricots to stretch velour, double knit, and terrycloth, fiber content will determine the handling.

These fabrics are soft, body-hugging, and vary in flexibility. Plushy knits can be both dense and revealing. A soft silhouette is the trademark of very stretchy knits.

## Priorities

Single knits require special handling to prevent snagging and pulling. Give extra consideration to the pile and nap of heavier, thick-surfaced knits. Handle stretch knits carefully to prevent stretching.

**Under Fabrics:** Underlining is unnecessary. Use interfacing only when absolutely necessary; it is generally eliminated for turtlenecks and soft collars. Lining is also taboo, but if your knit is too revealing, make a slip of taffeta or satin.

**Fabric Preparation:** Grain perfection is important, so straighten fabric if necessary. Pre-shrink washable stretch knits.

**Alterations and Fitting:** Refer to page 11 for pattern alterations. As a precaution, add 1" wide seam allowances if you feel your garment may be too clinging.

**Layout and Marking:** Because stretch knits have shading and one-way designs, see page 11 before laying out your pattern. Cut and mark as you would a velvet (page 17). Tailor's tacks or pins and chalk are suggested for these fabrics.

## Construction

Construction techniques for stretch knits are essentially the same as those for jerseys.

**Pressing:** Stretch knits should be pressed like jerseys to prevent imprints of the seam allowances. Plushy velours and terrycloth require a needleboard, self-fabric press pad, or Turkish towel to protect pile, ribs, and raised designs.

**Seams:** A preliminary to seaming stretch knits is SPECIALIZED HAND BASTING. Pin garment sections together and baste vertical seams loosely with lengths of doubled thread—baste from the top toward lower edge of your garment. To start, fasten end securely; make a single backstitch to end each length, leaving about 12" of thread dangling. Try on the garment and distribute the fabric along each basting thread until wrinkles and pulls disappear; adjust seam allowances if necesary. Re-baste and check fit.

Stretch knit seams are handled as suggested for jerseys (page 41).

**Closures:** Select a zipper that is as short and lightweight as possible. When fitting, pin sides of closure to zipper tape; stretch as necessary and baste. Stretch and smooth fabric as you stitch zipper in place. Closure areas wrinkle when knit garments are not worn.

**Hems:** Hems must have flexibility; edgestitch hem edge and double catchstitch hem (page 41).

**Care:** Washables should be laundered according to hang-tag or end of bolt instructions. For storage, use padded hangers, make tape hangers (page 23), or fold the garment in tissue paper.

# Special Attention Fabrics

Tiny, medium-size, and wide ribbed fabrics come in a variety of fibers, weights, and degrees of softness and crispness. Faille, ottoman, Bedford cord, grosgrain, and corduroy are a few of these fabrics.

Cashmere is perhaps the most famous of luxury fibers, and certainly deserves particular notice. It is used to produce soft, napped fabrics in many weights.

Ribbed fabrics come in many weights, including the lightest faille and the heaviest ottoman. Choose ribbed fabrics to suit your needs: light- to medium weights can produce a supple evening gown or a clinging casual outfit, while the heavyweights can create jackets, coats, and multi-purpose cover-ups with distinctive character. Like stripes, fabrics with pronounced crosswise ribs appear to add girth to both your design and figure—plan their use carefully. Many soft ribbed fabrics—especially knits—can be quite figure-revealing; be sure to use them to your best advantage.

## Priorities

When the ribbed fabric you've selected has characteristics like those of other special fabrics already discussed, refer to those sections for additional information. Ribbed fabrics like chenille, corduroy, ottoman, and bengaline are treated much like fabrics with nap, pile, and one-way designs. Similarly, lightweight faille and grosgrain are related to taffeta.

**Under Fabrics:** Let your fabric and pattern determine the amount of support your design needs from under fabrics. Select under fabrics which have care requirements like those of your fashion fabric.

**Fabric Preparation:** See the fabric preparation section (page 10) for details on straightening the grain which can be applied to ribbed fabrics. Pre-shrink your fabric as for velvets (pages 16-17), omitting the shower-steaming process.

**Alterations and Fitting:** If your ribbed fabric is woven, this can be accomplished as for velvet (page 17). Stretch ribbed fabrics should be altered according to the instructions on page 42 for stretch knits.

CASHMERE
CORDUROY

## Ribbed Fabrics

Fiber content and construction determine the extent of special handling required. Ribbed fabrics can be soft or crisp—from body-hugging knitted velours and sweater ribs to sturdy woven poplins, bengalines, and corduroys.

**Layouts:** Your fabric may have shading and call for a "With Nap" layout (page 11). Like stripes, large and prominent ribs should be matched—align them at seamlines before cutting out garment.

**Marking:** Mark soft plushy ribs as you would velvet—with tailor's tacks, or pins and chalk. Depending on the fabric, some flat crisp ribs may be marked with a tracing wheel and dressmaker's tracing paper.

## Construction

Fabrics containing wool and cotton often can withstand more handling than those containing silk, nylon, or other man-made fibers.

**Pressing:** Press most wool, cotton, and man-made fiber ribbed fabrics with a steam iron. Soft, delicate ribbed fabrics are pressed like lace fabrics (see pages 21-22 for details).

**Seams:** For soft ribs with pile, use the same seams as you would for velvets (pages 17-18). Crisp lightweight failles, poplins, and Bedford cords can be stitched much like satin (pages 25-26); use polyester or silk thread to prevent puckering.

**Closures:** Practically any closure you might desire will be appropriate for medium to heavyweight ribbed fabrics. In lightweight silk or man-made fiber ribbed fabrics, avoid zippers and buttonholes. Refer to the closures for sheer fabrics (page 29) and laces (page 22).

**Hems:** Medium to heavyweight rib fabrics, particularly if soft and napped, may require a soft hem and may need interfacing for support (see page 9). A narrow hem or narrow horsehair braid hem works well with some lightweight ribbed fabrics (see pages 29-30). Knitted light- or medium weight ribbed fabrics often require a double catchstitched hem (see page 41).

**Care:** Weight, weave, and fiber determine the kind of care to be given your fabric; read hang-tag or end of bolt for this information. Stretchy ribbed fabrics will benefit from the use of a padded hanger and tape hangers (page 23).

# Cashmere

Cashmere is the ultimate fine, soft, fleecy fabric. Although many other fibers are used to simulate the properties of this fine hair, the quality of cashmere is far above any imitation. However, fabrics resembling cashmere—like kasha, a cotton flannel having a twill weave on one side—are handled like cashmere in preparation and construction. Do not be deterred by the price of pure cashmere—if high quality delights you, the fabric will be well worth the expense. Cashmere is not difficult to handle; you must simply be aware of it. Fiber content controls special handling to some extent—fabrics with some cashmere may be less delicate. Cashmere can be soft or crisp, depending on the fibers blended with it, the fabric type, and structure.

This versatile fabric is found in many weights—from light, almost tissue paper thin to heavy coating. Depending on the weave or knit of your fabric, its weight, density, and drape demand consideration.

## Priorities

**Under Fabrics:** Most cashmeres can be underlined, interfaced, and lined in the traditional way.

**Fabric Preparation, Alterations and Fitting, Layouts, and Marking:** Follow the instructions given for velvets, pages 16-17. The expense of this fabric warrants making a muslin first.

## Construction

All techniques—**Pressing, Seams, Closures, Hems, and Care**—are like those for velvets; however, omit shower steaming.

# Trimmings and Surface Interest

Make special fabrics extra special by adding a personal trimming touch to your fashions. Smocking, shirring, quilting, and tucking will add surface interest to your garment. These trims must be applied before you cut out your fabric. Trims applied during the construction of your garment or added to the finished design include appliqués, beads, sequins, embroidery, braids, bands, and feathers. Either approach to trimming can make your fashion unique in an instant.

## Before You Cut...

Add surface interest to garment areas with smocking, shirring, quilting, and tucking. These must be prepared before cutting out your pattern, as they require more fabric than is allowed by the pattern piece. Following are suggestions and ideas you can use to create a special look for your garment. The Vogue Sewing Book and "Everything About Sewing Trims" from Vogue Patterns offer you the particulars of construction details.

**Smocking** is a form of shaping —try it for a special effect on a waistline, yoke, cuff, or entire bodice. Smocking can be done by hand or machine with embroidery floss or elastic thread. Reserve smocking for those soft fabrics which can withstand the extra handling of the extensive marking and stitching involved. Fabrics like lightweight crepe, batiste, jersey, tricot, georgette, dotted Swiss, and crepe-back satin may be smocked in a very small stitch pattern. Medium weight soft fabrics like velveteen, knitted velour, velvet, and crepe can be smocked, but only in a stitch pattern large enough to accommodate their bulk. Experiment on fabric scraps first.

**Shirring** is a decorative form of gathering. Several types of shirring can be done in a variety of ways. Shirring is effective only on soft or very lightweight fabrics like those used for intricate smocking. Use shirring to snug in a waistline or cuff, or simply to decorate garment areas of your choice.

**Quilting** can be a beautiful addition to a satin collar on a velvet blazer or to a full length skirt. Quilt small areas of your fashion — like cuffs and bands—or quilt the whole garment! Experiment with a layer of cotton wadding, polyester fleece, or very thin foam rubber sandwiched between the fashion fabric and underlining. Quilt your own design or outline a fabric design by hand or machine. Velveteen, satin, velvet, backed lace, and brocade are fabrics enhanced by quilting.

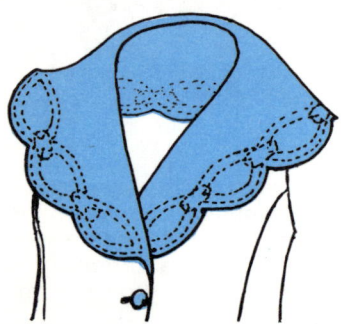

**Tucking** is a versatile addition used to create surface interest or to control fullness and shape your fashion contour. Decorative tucks are slender folds, usually on the straight grain of the fabric, stitched from the right side. The color of thread, and the depth and direction of the tucks are the design variables. Test the many kinds of tucks on some fabric samples. Try tucking pieces of your special fabric, then working them into a patchwork design for a smashing skirt or vest. Many flat fabrics — soft or crisp — are easily tucked and decorated by this simple procedure.

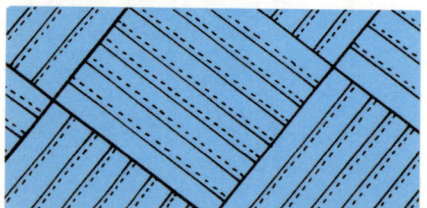

# Add-Ons

Decorative touches added to your garment include appliqués, beads, sequins, embroidery, braids, and bands. The possibilities are literally never-ending, what with all the different trims available. When putting these trims on special fabrics, be certain that your fabric can withstand the additional weight of the trim and the extra handling it requires. These trims can be applied to your fabric either by hand or machine — set your creativity to work, and have fun placing them on your garment.

**Appliqués,** purchased or handmade, are separate pieces of fabric applied to a larger background. For example, lace appliqués might consist of motifs of the lace on a contrasting fabric. Or, you can cut your own motif from a fabric and appliqué it to your special fabric.

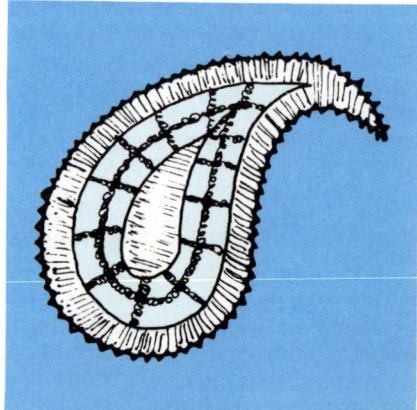

**Beads** can be attached to your fabric creation singly, in groups, or in a continuous strand. By attaching beads or rhinestones singly, you can create a random pattern which adds the perfect amount of refined zest to your fabric. Or, create a work of art by beading an entire garment area like a yoke, cuffs, or inset band. Bead loops and fringe can combine several different shapes and colors of beads to produce an ornate, eye-catching garment edge.

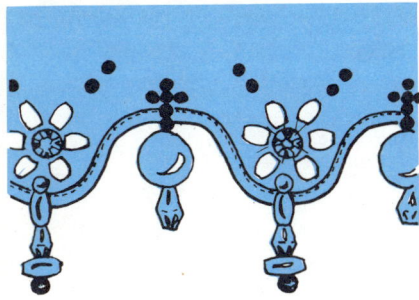

ordinary effect. Or, combine embroidery stitches with beads, seed pearls, sequins, or rhinestones.

**Sequins** come in all sizes, shapes, and colors, and may be purchased singly, in a continuous strand, or as a band. They make a stunning textural trim when combined with a small bead. To avoid over-handling your special fabric, make an appliqué of sequins on a workable fabric and sew this finished motif to your garment.

**Braids, Bands, and Feathers,** found in countless colors, widths, and styles are the easiest trims to apply, but the most difficult to select! Weight is important—your fabric must be able to support the trim without strain or pulling. Flat and soutache braids, ribbon and embroidered bands, fold-over braids, bindings, pipings, cordings, and rickrack—in short, any trim your heart desires—are available in trim form. These can be used for edgings at necks, sleeves, hems; at waistlines or placket fronts; and even to camouflage a zipper.

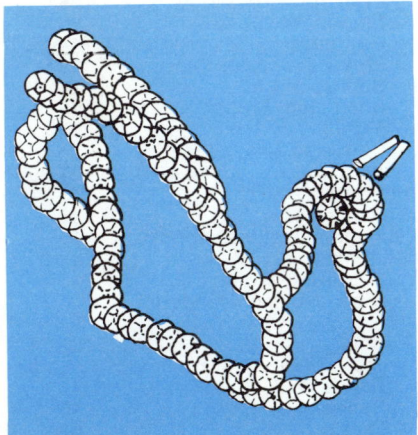

**Embroidery** is perhaps the most personal of all trims—particularly if stitched by hand. Your fabric should be sturdy if you plan to use an embroidery hoop. Pile or napped fabrics may be too easily crushed. Embroidery floss is the traditional medium of embroidered design, but you may substitute angora yarn or metallic threads for an out-of-the-

# Index

Alterations .................. 11
  (See also specific fabric)
Appliqués .................. 46

Backing .................... 9
Basting .................. 12-13
  Specialized Hand (for knits) .42
Beaded Fabrics ............ 38-39
Brocade .................. 34-35

Care
  Tape Hangers ............ 23
  Tissue Paper Support ...... 26
  (See also specific fabric)
Cashmere .................. 44
Closures
  Continuous Lap Opening .... 29
  (See also specific fabric)
Crepe .................... 30-32

Embroidery ................ 47

Fabric Preparation ........ 10-11
  (See also specific fabric)
Fabric Selection ........... 7-8
Fitting .................... 11

Handstitches .............. 13-14
  Backstitch ................ 13
  Blindstitch ................ 14
  Catchstitch ............... 13
  Half Backstitch ........... 13
  Hemming Stitch .......... 14
  Prickstitch ................ 13
  Running Stitch ........... 14
  Slipstitch ................. 13
Hem Finishes
  Lace Scallops ............. 23
  Narrow Horsehair Braid .... 30
  Net Facing ............... 23
  Padded .................. 26
  Wide Horsehair Braid ...... 35
  (See also specific fabric)
Hems
  Curved ................ 33-34
  Double-Catchstitched ...... 41
  Faced .................... 37
  Hand-Rolled .............. 29
  Interfaced ................ 18
  Lace Trim (edge finish) .... 22
  Machine .................. 29
  Narrow .................. 29
  Wire .................... 30
  (See also specific fabric)

Interfacing ................. 9

Knits .................... 40-42
  Jersey ................. 40-41
  Stretch ................ 41-42

Laces .................... 19-23

Layouts .................. 11-12
  (See also specific fabric)
Lining .................... 10
  (See also specific fabric)

Machine Sewing ............ 14
Marking .................. 12
  (See also specific fabric)
Metallics ................ 36-37

Pattern Selection and Sizes ... 6
Pressing
  Finger-Pressing .......... 36-37
  (See also specific fabric)

Quilting .................. 46

Ribbed Fabrics ............ 43-44

Satin .................... 24-26
Seam Finishes
  Bound .................. 18
  Hong Kong ............. 25-26
  Stitched and Overcast .... 17
  Zigzag .................. 18
Seams .................... 14-15
  Appliquéing Lace ......... 22
  Enclosed ................ 22
  French .................. 28
  French Whipped .......... 28
  Gathered .............. 14-15
  Piped .................... 37
  Self-Bound .............. 28
  Simulated French ........ 28
  Taped .................. 15
  (See also specific fabric)
Sheers .................. 27-30
Shirring .................. 45
Smocking ................ 45
Stay (for waistline support) .... 19
Stiffening ................ 9-10
Suporting Ruffle .......... 33
  (See also specifc fabric)

Taffeta .................. 32-34
Trims
  Bands .................. 47
  Beads .................. 46
  Braids .................. 47
  Feathers ................ 47
  Sequins ................ 47
Tucking .................. 46

Underlining ................ 9
  (See also specific fabric)

Velvet .................. 16-19

Yardage .................. 8
  Conversion Chart .......... 8

Zippers (See specific fabric)